"Eleanor Roosevelt changed the world with her leadership. Robin Gerber tells us how she did it, weaving the first lady's life story and words into empowering leadership advice for today. . . . [A] great read and a terrific leadership guide."—**Lt. General Claudia Kennedy**

"This book is a terrific read; it tells Eleanor's story with descriptive flair and gives readers wise advice about finding their leadership passion and following it."—**Billie Jean King**

"Without a doubt, Eleanor Roosevelt was one the greatest leaders in American history. Robin Gerber clearly demonstrates why in this superb, lucid, and compelling study. It is a joy to read."—**Donald T. Phillips,** *Lincoln on Leadership*

"This inspiring book shows Eleanor Roosevelt the leader, a woman who transformed her time. Her legacy, as Robin Gerber illustrates, is a road map to leadership for women today."—**Congresswoman Nancy Pelosi, House Democratic Whip**

"Eleanor Roosevelt's leadership made her first lady of the world. She's the perfect model for the leadership advice and ideas contained in this fascinating and insightful book."—**Congressman Steny Hoyer, Co-Chair House Democratic Steering Committee**

"Eleanor Roosevelt's life and leadership provide the inspiration; Robin Gerber provides the how-to. This wise and wonderful book should be required reading for all women (and men) on their way up."—**Judy B. Rosener, Ph.D.,** *Ways Women Lead*

"Robin Gerber has crafted the perfect primer to an extraordinary life and the ideal motivational tool for Everywoman to become a leader through the deliberate use of her own unique experiences and opportunities. Whether one reads this book for historic information, for behavior strategies, or for motivation, one will not be disappointed."—**Jadwiga S. Sebrechts, President, Women's College Coalition, Washington, D.C.**

"Eleanor Roosevelt was a great leader on many fronts, but especially in the fight for racial equality. This book gives readers a true feeling for the former first lady's conviction, her courage, and her passion for leadership. It's an inspirational story, and Robin Gerber uses it expertly to give advice to anyone hoping to lead."—**Congresswoman Stephanie Tubbs Jones**

"A lot of people admire Eleanor Roosevelt but don't understand her leadership strengths. She was a great strategist, knew how to engage people, and loved to compete. This book gives readers fast-paced, on-target advice on how to do the same."—**Julie Foudy, U.S. Women's National Soccer Team Captain, Olympic Gold Medalist, World Cup Champion, and President of the Women's Sports Foundation**

"Eleanor Roosevelt is a powerful role model for women leaders. In this book, Robin Gerber gleans leadership lessons from Eleanor's life story and weaves them into an easy-to-use guidebook for leaders of today and tomorrow."—**Kathy Whitmire, Mayor of Houston 1982-1992**

"An inspiring book based on the values and leadership style of one of the most inspirational women of all time. A must read for anyone interested in improving their leadership skills."—**Jacci Duncan, Executive Director, National Association of Women Business Owners**

"Robin Gerber has spotted the critical experiences which define the drive and insight of Eleanor Roosevelt's leadership. Leaders of organizations, communities, and families will find that each chapter offers practical insights and recommendations. Highly recommended!"— **Connie Rath, Vice Chair and Dean, Gallup University**

"Despite her fears and doubts, Eleanor Roosevelt refused to alienate herself from the plight of discriminated people. We can learn much from this book which captures the great power and unconquerable spirit of Eleanor Roosevelt."—**Margaret Daniels Tyler, McKinsey & Company**

"This book is a classic leadership 'how-to-do' for women of all ages."—**Mary Elcano, Partner, Sidley Austin Brown & Wood**

"With a fresh eye and highly original insight, Robin Gerber tells the stirring story of the legendary Eleanor Roosevelt's transformation from pathetic child to world figure and combines it with detailed how-to advice for developing personal leadership. The result is a unique book that will connect an icon of the past to a new generation seeking leadership at every level."— **Bonnie Angelo, Author,** *First Mothers: The Women Who Shaped the Presidents*

"Robin Gerber has fashioned the life of one of the world's truly great women into a beautiful, inspiring and most important useful meditation on the ways that all women can discover the greatness and the power within themselves."—**Marita Golden, President, The Zora Neale Hurston/Richard Wright Foundation**

"Eleanor Roosevelt knew how tough it was to lead from the White House or your own house. this book shows why she is a great role model for the many women who still don't see their own potential."—**Marie C. Wilson, President, The White House Project**

"Women today can learn so much from Eleanor Roosevelt's life and leadership. Robin Gerber makes it fun, delivering compelling lessons with wisdom, clarity, and style."— **Celinda Lake, President, Lake Snell Perry Associates, Democratic Pollsters**

"This book gives practical and inspiring advice on how to be a leader. It's a great resource for anyone who wants to develop and improve leadership strategies and to learn about an amazing woman in the process."—**Robin Gradison, Emmy Award-Winning Producer for ABC News**

"Like Mohandas Gandhi or Martin Luther King, Jr., Eleanor Roosevelt seems a miracle of character and charisma, a born leader whom no one could hope to emulate. Robin Gerber penetrates this aura, however powerful, and exposes the nuts and bolts of an eminently practical leadership style—one from which we can all learn and learn much."
—**Alan Axelrod, Author,** *Patton on Leadership* **and** *Elizabeth I, CEO*

"Eleanor Roosevelt challenged all of us to listen, think, act, build coalitions, and dream—to lead. This book helps us pick up where she left off."—**Allida Black, The Eleanor Roosevelt Papers, The George Washington University**

"Eleanor Roosevelt comes alive in this book in all her vulnerability, courage, and strength. Robin Gerber turns an icon into a woman and allows us to see ourselves in ER's experience and to draw courage to be more than we are. . . . [A] transformational reading experience."—**Melody Woolley, Girls Leadership Workshop Coordinator, Eleanor Roosevelt Center at Val-Kill**

". . . Filled with practical examples of how one woman, working with creativity and diligence, can make a huge difference. An inspiring how-to for women to exert leadership at every stage of life."—**Margaret Engel, Managing Editor, The Newseum**

Leadership the Eleanor Roosevelt Way

Timeless Strategies from the First Lady of Courage

Robin Gerber

Prentice Hall Press

A member of Penguin Putnam Inc.
375 Hudson Street
New York, N.Y. 10014
www.penguinputnam.com

Prentice Hall® is a registered trademark of Pearson Education, Inc.

All photographs are courtesy of the Franklin D. Roosevelt Library and Digital Archives.

Library of Congress Cataloging-in-Publication Data

Gerber, Robin.
    Leadership the Eleanor Roosevelt way / Robin Gerber.
        p.   cm.
    Includes bibliographical references (p.) and index.
    ISBN 0-7352-0324-5
    1. Roosevelt, Eleanor, 1884–1962.   2. Presidents' spouses—United States—Biography.   3. Leadership—United States.   I. Title.

E807.1.R48.G47   2002
973.917′092—dc21   2002066763
    [B]

Page Design by Robyn Beckerman

Printed in the United States of America
10 9 8 7 6 5 4 3 2

For my father, Sam Gerber
1913–1986

Foreword

James MacGregor Burns

*D*ear Reader: I begin in this infor-
mal way because I want to establish direct contact with you,
for I want you to know that this book is not only about
Eleanor Roosevelt—it is about *you*—your possible hopes and
aspirations, your potential, perhaps even your future. If you
are simply interested in reading more about the life of a great
leader, though, I can tell you that this is one of the finest por-
traits of Eleanor Roosevelt I have read.

But this volume offers even more—a direct connection
between her life and what could be yours. For above all,
Eleanor Roosevelt stands as a role model, because of the way
she rose out of "patrician adversity," lost a beloved father,
encountered many obstacles, and went on to a life filled with
adventures and some misadventures. I have never read a
biography that, page after page, connects the subject so inti-
mately with the daily needs and hopes, opportunities and
ambitions of readers especially of young women seeking the
best of all role models. (This book is written mainly for
women, but men can read it profitably, too.)

How was Eleanor Roosevelt a great leader? She exemplified the qualities of leadership that scholars have identified
as crucial. First of all, she responded to people's fundamental

wants and needs—especially those who are disadvantaged. Second, because she was innovative and creative in her ideas about how we can improve not only our own lives but also those around us. Third, because she knew that to fight for grand but controversial principles meant that inevitably one comes into conflict with others, and she never shrank from a grand fight for principle. But above all—as this book insists— she was an outstanding leader because of her ethical standards and her values: She believed in ethical conduct both in public and private life and she believed in the great principles that have guided America from the start (summed up in the glowing words of the Declaration of Independence, "life, liberty and the pursuit of happiness" and its commitment to equality).

In short, I have never read a book that more skillfully intertwines the story of Eleanor Roosevelt's life with daily, down-to-earth lessons for us all. Neither Eleanor Roosevelt nor Robin Gerber preaches to us—they teach by example.

No more now, because you should get right to the book. But since this work is so rich in anecdotes, I wish to add my own personal experience with the qualities of Eleanor Roosevelt that are brilliantly limned in this work. Years ago, when I was an intern in Washington, the whole intern group received word out of the blue that Eleanor Roosevelt had invited us to supper at the White House. We were the lowliest of the low in Washington—unpaid and overworked—and of course that was the main reason she invited us! We were elated. But as the time for the visit neared we became apprehensive—this was 1939–40 and tension was rising day by day after Hitler's conquest of Poland. Security was tight—surely, our visit would be cancelled. But, of course, it was not. And we had the most memorable evening of our lives as we gathered around to hear her talk in much the same fashion as Robin Gerber has captured in this book.

I happened to be living with other interns only a block and a half from the White House. When we gathered on the sidewalk, Arista Sarkus, a very poor immigrant girl from New Jersey, hailed a cab. "Arista," I cried out, "what are you doing? It's just around the corner, and a cab will cost 20 cents and a nickel tip!" "Never mind," she said, drawing herself up to her full five feet. "All my life I've wanted to call a taxi and say, 'The White House please!' And of course what made it special—it was Eleanor Roosevelt's White House.

Preface

*S*ix years ago, an intriguing title caught my eye as I was killing time at an airport bookstore. *Lincoln on Leadership*, by Donald T. Phillips, seemed to be a clever twist on the books I studied as a faculty member at the Academy of Leadership at the University of Maryland. I bought it as a quick, informative read, and I wasn't disappointed. Only later did I find out that the book had launched a small industry of similar titles in the business leadership book genre.

As a historian and leadership educator, I thought Phillips did a terrific job of weaving Lincoln stories and quotes around principles of leadership for today's executives. But I wanted something more. My area of expertise is women's leadership, particularly in politics and business. Surely there were some women leaders who could offer leadership wisdom, I thought. So I started searching the book lists. I found *Patton on Leadership*, Robert E. Lee, Ulysses S. Grant, Jesus, Churchill, Gandhi, Martin Luther King, Jr., Ernest Shackleton, the Founding Fathers, and Ronald Reagan. But the only woman in the group was Elizabeth I. That's how this book was born.

I decided to write the book as a biography, analyzing the leadership lessons in each part of Eleanor's life, not only because Eleanor's transformation is inspiring, but also because women respond to the narrative of whole lives. We talk to each other about all aspects of our lives, weaving that knowledge into an elaborate pattern of relationships that crosses the boundaries of family and work. Thanks to the wise advice of my editor, I also included my personal stories and those of women today (some names are changed where the interviewee faced negative repercussions at work), which I hope will bring immediacy and greater relevance to the leadership advice.

This is a book that combines history and leadership advice. I owe an enormous debt to the fine historians who have chronicled Eleanor's life. The detailed biographies of Joseph Lash, the thoroughness and insight of Blanche Wiesen Cook's two volumes on Eleanor, the scholarly analysis of Allida Black's books, the elegant histories of James MacGregor Burns, and (despite the recent uproar over her earlier work on the Kennedys) the conclusions drawn by Doris Kearns Goodwin about Eleanor's impact on the country. All were of indispensable value to me.

Similarly, the scholars and other authors who have done leadership research and provided thoughtful analysis gave me a powerful foundation to build on.

This was particularly true of Burns's seminal work *Leadership* and the books of the late John W. Gardner. I relied a great deal on the ideas of women scholars like Rosabeth Moss Kanter, Helen Astin, Carol Gilligan, Karin Klenke, Judy Rosener, Sally Helgesen, and Jean Lipman-Blumen, who have broken much ground on women's leadership. But these brilliant women have just uncovered the tip of the iceberg when it comes to research and theory on women's leadership. More needs to be done, particularly as women move in growing numbers into leadership positions in our society. The study referenced in chapter three on mothering and leadership by the Wellesley Centers for Women is a good example of an area that will, I hope, be more fully explored in coming years.

There is one person whose intellect, passion, and insight were indispensable to this book—Eleanor Roosevelt. I found myself repeatedly astounded by her prescience, the contemporary power of her words and the compelling effect of her straightforward language. Her greatest gift is the written legacy she left the world—literally thousands of pages of letters, articles, books, speeches. (Thanks to the Internet we can even watch a brief snippet of her interviewing John F. Kennedy on her talk show in the 1960s.) Over time, as I read and reread Eleanor's words, learned more about her life, and thought about the implications for women leaders today, I found myself transformed. Writing this book changed me. It deepened my passion and resolve to continue a lifetime of working for women's equality in this culture. Eleanor led me to reflect on my leadership, focus on my passion, and get "fired up" about acting on it. I'd like to think that, if she were here, she would see this book as an acknowledgment of her leadership, a tribute to her accomplishments, and a heartfelt thank you.

Robin Gerber

Acknowledgments

Two people are responsible for launching me into the world of publishing. Georgia Sorenson, founder of the Academy of Leadership at the University of Maryland, encouraged my vision of changing my career and offered me the opportunity to write as part of the Academy faculty. Thanks to her I had the incomparable opportunity of working with James MacGregor Burns. His generous support, encouragement, and advice ("write books, books last," "Persistence, persistence, persistence") made this book possible.

Getting from idea to book takes the help of special people. First, my thanks to my friend, the fine essayist, Pamela Toutant. She has encouraged me in many ways and has been a brilliant collaborator on all my writing. She insisted that I attend the writers' conference where I met the wonderful Marita Golden, author and arts activist, whose first words to me were, "Do you have an agent, because I know the right woman if you don't." And that's how I met Lynn Whittaker. She provided patience, care, and professionalism as she helped shape the proposal and engaged in a masterful campaign to find a publisher. Thanks to her hard work I had the good fortune to get Ellen Schneid Coleman as my editor.

Experienced, wise, and astute (and a great fan of ER), Ellen's advice was unfailingly on target. I have felt completely secure in her able hands and fortunate to have found a new friend. My thanks as well to her able colleague, Yvette Romero, and the team at Penguin Putnam: Adrian Zackheim, Will Weisser, Elissa Altman, and Mark Ippoliti. My thanks as well to Barbara Lombardo and Barbara Monteiro for their enthusiasm in publicizing this book.

Writing the book took an enormous support network, but none more important than that provided by my colleagues at the Academy of Leadership. Staff, board, and senior fellows are all a continual source of support and intellectual challenge. I thank them all, but in particular the following: Nance Lucas, the director, has been an enthusiastic champion, scholarly resource, and encouraging friend; Stephanie Weiss, an incomparable editor and gifted writer in her own right, has influenced every page of this book, literally and intellectually. I can't thank her enough. Tracey Manning consistently offered scholarly advice and practical insights that improved the manuscript immeasurably. Connie Rath added her superb insight. Cheryl Ross gave excellent assistance.

Certain editors and writers have been of invaluable help as I developed as a writer. Thanks to Glen Nishimura, Chris Collins, and Carol Stevens at *USA Today*, Bill O'Sullivan at the *Washingtonian*, and Peter Milius of the *Washington Post*, who left this earth far too soon. Authors Peter Range, James Reston, Jr., Jay Winik, and Lyric Wallwork Winik have offered advice and encouragement. Sarah Priestman, a fine writer, has also been a dedicated friend and adviser, helping me over many rough spots. Peggy Engel always goes the extra hundred miles. Richard Whitmire has been the most enthusiastic of friends, creative, smart, and also a terrific writer. Special thanks to author Kitty Kelley, whose unbounded creativity and advice about the book world have been invaluable. Author and scholar Judy Rosener dropped into this project like an angel. Thanks also to friends and writers Susan Land, a novelist; screenwriter and long-lost friend Ilana Bar-Din Giannini; the fabulous Brooke Foster and Cynthia Chertos.

I am grateful to have many friends, but even more grateful for their patience, encouragement, and boundless support for this book and my writing life. Cindy Hallberlin, Anne Maher, Robin Gradison, Peggy McCormick, and Lisa Stevenson have borne the brunt of my ups and downs, and been steadfast beyond the call of friendship. Huge thanks as well to Mary Lu Jordan, Ben Elliott, Lisa Dobbs, Joan Kristal, Jeannie Pfaelzer, Sheila Feinberg, Chris Palmer, Peter Franchot, Norman Adler, Bob Powers, Jim Kolb, Kristi Daniels, Starr Ezra, Carol Beach, Lissa Muscatine, Linda Harris, Nancy Greenspan, Francine Levinson, Carol Green, Bob Snyder, Nancy Golding, Nicki Heidepriem, Audrey and Bob Bredhoff, Joe Petrone, Geri Palast, Liz Siegel, Sylvia Fubini, Rose Schwartz, my teammates on Shooting Stars, Earthquakes, and especially Vintage Lightning where I got my soccer start, and the wonderful staff and board members of Imagination Stage.

This would be a book of blank pages without the love, patience, and support of my family. My thanks to my mother for her delight in my accomplishments, to my sister, Dee Francken, for critique and inspiration, to my brother, Steve Gerber, for indefatigable cheerleading, and to my nephew James Francken whose wisdom about writing reveals his destiny.

Finally, I owe far more than I can express to my husband, Tony Records. He leads through love. My children are everyday miracles—Ariel, whose leadership will enrich our world through the dramatic arts, and Sam, understanding, smart, and kind, a leader of the next generation. All three have suffered my writing pains with humor, patience, and love.

Contents

CONTENTS

Time Line

Oct. 11, 1884   Elliot and Anna Roosevelt have their first child, Anna Eleanor.

1892   Eleanor's mother dies of diphtheria. Eleanor and brothers, Elliott Jr. and Hall, go to live with Anna's mother.

1893   Eleanor's brother Elliott Jr. dies at the age of four.

1894   Eleanor's father dies of the effects of alcoholism and addiction.

1899   Eleanor goes to study with Marie Souvestre at Allenswood, a girls' school outside of London.

1902   Eleanor leaves Allenswood and returns to New York to make her debut in society.

1905   Eleanor marries Franklin Delano Roosevelt.

1906   Eleanor has her first child and only girl, Anna.

1907   Eleanor has her second child, James.

1909   Eleanor has her third child, Franklin Jr., who dies in infancy.

1910   Eleanor has her fourth child, Elliott. Franklin is elected to state office, and the family moves to Albany, New York.

1913	Franklin becomes assistant secretary of the Navy and the family moves to Washington, D.C.
1914	Eleanor has her fifth child, Franklin Jr.
1916	Eleanor has her last child, John, a year before the United States enters World War I.
1918	Eleanor discovers Franklin's affair with Lucy Mercer.
1920	Franklin nominated as vice-presidential running mate to James N. Cox. Eleanor accompanies Franklin on campaign trail. Cox/FDR lose to Republicans Warren G. Harding and Calvin Coolidge.
1921	Franklin contracts polio.
1922–1928	Eleanor becomes increasingly active in Democratic politics; Franklin is elected governor of New York in 1928.
1932	Franklin is elected president of the United States.
1933	Eleanor holds her first women-only press conference as first lady. She begins her "My Day" column.
1936	Franklin is reelected.
1940	Eleanor speaks on Franklin's behalf at the Democratic convention. He wins an unprecedented third term.
1941	Japan bombs Pearl Harbor, and the United States enters World War II.
1943	Eleanor visits U.S. troops in the South Pacific.

1945   Eleanor joins the NAACP board of directors after years of work to secure greater civil rights for African Americans. In April, Franklin dies. In September, World War II ends with the surrender of Japan.

1946   Eleanor begins drafting the Universal Declaration of Human Rights as head of the United Nations Human Rights Commission.

1948   The Human Rights Declaration is passed by the United Nations.

1950   Eleanor begins work on television and radio with NBC studios.

1952   Eleanor supports Adlai Stevenson for president, but he loses to Eisenhower.

1960   Eleanor gives John F. Kennedy her support for the presidency.

Nov. 7, 1962 Eleanor dies at the age of seventy-eight.

Introduction

*E*leanor Roosevelt holds an unassailable place as the most respected and well-known woman of the last century. In the years before her death in 1962, international polls repeatedly showed her to be the world's most admired woman. Her renowned biographer, Blanche Wiesen Cook, says that today, "Young people seem to know nothing about history, but they know Eleanor Roosevelt. Everywhere I go, people are galvanized and energized by her."

Eleanor's life has inspired biographies, compilations of her writing, and countless posthumous honors and buildings named after her. In all of these contexts she is called a leader, and rightfully so. Yet nowhere will you find an analysis of her leadership. No book has culled out the values, strategies, tactics, and beliefs that allowed her to bring about transformational change.

I wrote this book because the most important part of Eleanor Roosevelt's legacy for women today is understanding Eleanor as a leader and discovering what she believed were the hallmarks of powerful leadership.

Take one of the best known stories about Eleanor as an example of what we know and yet haven't fully explored about her. In 1939, the African American opera singer Marian

Anderson planned a concert in Washington, D.C. The Daughters of the American Revolution, of which Eleanor was a member, refused to let Anderson sing at DAR Constitution Hall, and they made their reasons plain. "No Negro will ever sing here," the DAR president announced to the press. In response, Eleanor captured worldwide attention by publicly resigning in protest from the group. "You had an opportunity to lead in an enlightened way," she wrote to the DAR president, "and your organization has failed." Eleanor supported arrangements for Anderson to sing on the steps of the Lincoln Memorial. Then the first lady, in a remarkable and little known act of leadership, didn't go to the concert. She didn't join the 75,000 people who filled the mall and thrilled at hearing the great contralto sing the national anthem and "America." Why didn't Eleanor attend? She wanted the historic moment to belong to Anderson, and she knew her own presence would be a distraction.

Decisiveness and bold action. Character built on firm values. Support for the leadership of others. By the end of her husband's second term, these pillars of Eleanor's leadership style were firmly in place. But without a position of formal authority (Eleanor didn't become U.N. delegate until 1945), whom did Eleanor lead?

Psychologist and author Howard Gardner compared Eleanor to Martin Luther King, Jr. They were both, in Gardner's words, "leaders of nondominant groups . . . leaders of the dispossessed." But the dispossessed find it hard to act as leaders because they feel alone. "Isolation," author

Margaret Wheatley writes, "is one barrier to courageous action." Eleanor led by breaking down isolation, by bringing communities together, and by forging ties across racial and class lines. She showed extraordinary flexibility in her thinking along with adaptability to the vast changes that swept her life.

Gardner argues that Eleanor also led directly as an advocate of women's role in government, as a public voice for liberal issues, as an "ombudswoman" with federal agencies on behalf of the public, as an adviser to her husband, and as a prod on issues of social reform. And her leadership had results. As historian Doris Kearns Goodwin explains, after her husband's death, Eleanor "understood that much of her vision had been realized, that the war had become a vehicle for social reform at home. The United States had been transformed from a weak, isolationist, socially stratified country to a powerful, productive, prosperous society, more just than ever in its history."

But how had Eleanor become a leader for change? What were the events in her life that forged her leadership style? And what can women today learn from Eleanor's leadership development and her thoughts and words about leadership? These are the questions this book seeks to answer, because the life lessons that made Eleanor a transforming leader have uncommon power to inspire our own leadership.

Despite her hallowed historic status, Eleanor's path to leadership will be surprisingly familiar to any woman who has balanced love and ambition, who has struggled with fear of failure, and who understands the need to learn and grow. The lessons to be drawn from Eleanor's life apply to women exercising their leadership across sectors—from business to government to the nonprofit world. Eleanor would agree with such a broad application of her ideas despite her primary concern with social justice. She firmly believed and constantly advocated that women's leadership was important in every sphere. She saw her life as a continual process of breaking down barriers and moving toward new and greater goals. Her strategy and her strength came through leadership and through refining her ideas about motivating others in the pursuit of mutual goals and passions.

From the day she was born, Eleanor faced extraordinary obstacles that seemed to mitigate against her development as a leader. Her young parents were part of New York's high society, but their wealth and status brought little happiness to the household. Eleanor's mother was cold and removed, disappointed in her only daughter's lack of beauty and social graces. Eleanor's beloved father grew into an alcoholic and drug abuser, frequently absent from home and involved with other women. By her tenth birthday Eleanor was an orphan, having lost one parent to diphtheria and the other to the ravages of his addictions.

Eleanor lived with her maternal grandmother for four years until she sailed for England. There she spent three years at Allenswood, a school for girls run by the famed educator Marie Souvestre. At Allenswood, Eleanor's intellectual capability and curiosity blossomed. Souvestre became a trusted mentor and friend. Eleanor returned to New York interested in social change, and began working with immigrant women and at settlement houses. She had begun to turn a difficult childhood into a powerful belief in discipline, a set of values related to social change, and the beginnings of the inquisitiveness and collaboration that marked her leadership.

Eleanor's social work career in New York was short-lived. She and her distant cousin, Franklin Delano Roosevelt, fell in love and were married before her twenty-first birthday, in 1905. For the next dozen years Eleanor lived as a wife and mother. She bore six children, one of whom died in infancy. Like mothers today, Eleanor practiced her leadership as a parent, within the context of her times. Meanwhile, FDR launched his political career by going to the New York state senate in 1910. Living under the fierce dominance of her mother-in-law, Sara Delano, Eleanor struggled to define herself, her hopes, and her future. In 1917, World War I offered her a chance to exercise her leadership inclinations as she took on volunteer work for American soldiers.

A monumental turning point in Eleanor's life came in 1918, when she discovered that Franklin was having an affair with her social secretary, Lucy Mercer. Although Eleanor was heartbroken, she chose to reinvent her marriage rather than destroy it. She and Franklin formed a new kind of partnership that freed her emotionally and psychologically to pursue her leadership passions. The Lucy Mercer affair pushed Eleanor more powerfully toward a path she had started on during the war.

Eleanor aligned herself with a group of activist women who were fighting for suffrage and against the prejudices of the time. She spent the 1920s finding her own identity, causes, and collaborators. She also recommitted herself to FDR, helping him overcome polio and remain in the political arena. She laid the groundwork for her future leadership by developing diverse networks and testing herself as a speaker and political operative. She used her vision to develop projects that were in line with her values, such as the Val-Kill furniture factory to teach rural adults a skill for economic independence and the Todhunter School for Girls in New York City.

In 1933, Eleanor became a reluctant first lady, worried that she would lose the ability to pursue her agenda for social change. Once again she had to adjust to a new place, new role, and unprecedented events. She became at once a heroine and a target of hostile critics. But she also became her husband's eyes and ears, bringing him detailed stories of poverty in Appalachia, lynchings in the South, unemployment across the land, and the desperate plight of poor children in American cities and on American farms.

She pushed ahead with projects that would make real change in people's lives. Housing and community development became Eleanor's crusade as she took steps to create a model city called "Arthurdale" for the rural poor. She created her own bully pulpit to promote New Deal programs, starting a daily column called "My Day" that reached the tiniest towns and the largest cities. She did radio broadcasts and gave countless speeches. And she never stopped promoting opportunities for women—from holding press conferences exclusively for women journalists to supporting women for appointments to public office.

Eleanor's years in Washington were a proving ground for her leadership skills. In her role as first lady, she learned to get skin "as thick as a rhinoceros," control her press coverage, judge relationships, and set priorities. By the time FDR died in 1945, the "First Lady of the World" was ready to tackle global change and was appointed to the first U.S. delegation to the United Nations by President Truman. In 1947 Eleanor was elected to chair the U.N. Human Rights Commission, and she guided the drafting of the Universal Declaration of Human Rights. Her crowning achievement came in securing the passage of the Declaration by the General Assembly in 1948, bringing her lifelong vision of justice and humanity to the world.

Eleanor came to believe that learning and growing, remaining curious, and being open to change were essential elements of leadership. In her last years of life she was as active as she had been in her youth, and she fought against McCarthyism and for new civil right laws. She cemented her image in the public mind as an enduring force for change.

If there are essential threads that can be pulled from Eleanor's story of leadership, they are her adherence to her values, her keen assessment of people's needs, and her ability to motivate those around her to take responsibility and work for change. Starting from her childhood, this book builds on those key elements, explaining how they developed and where they led. It is Eleanor's story—a story that unfolds as a lasting gift to women leaders who still face many of the challenges Eleanor confronted.

In 2002, there are more women CEOs in the Fortune 1000 than ever before, but the total is still barely more than 1 percent. And these women face greater scrutiny and harsher penalties for failure than men do. Further, the 2000 census shows nearly equivalent numbers of women and men holding college degrees, yet 25 percent more men earn salaries greater than $75,000 a year. Studies released in 2002 by Congress and a group of women corporate executives and business owners confirm that equality for women in business is still a distant dream. Although women are starting businesses at much faster rates than men and actively breaking into the technology sector, their access to capital is severely limited. Women are also still grossly underrepresented in positions of power in politics. Women comprise only 13 percent of the members of Congress, and barely more than a fifth of all state legislators are female.

Although these issues differ somewhat in kind or degree from the problems of Eleanor's day, the solutions rest on the same foundation: leadership. Why? Leadership is about change. It means intentionally achieving a helpful, ethical purpose, and doing so in a process of reciprocal motivation and support between leaders and those they hope to lead. And although many aspects of society must change for women to achieve true equality of opportunity, women can start by making personal change. We can work to develop and exercise our leadership to achieve our individual visions of change—whether those visions are to build a business, win public office, reform the local PTA, raise good citizens, or move into top management in the private sector.

This book is my act of leadership, an attempt to motivate other women to be leaders through the powerful words and deeds of the greatest woman leader of our time. I hope it will encourage you to act, to challenge yourself, to believe enough in your dreams to turn them into reality. I hope you will discover, or further develop, the leadership you already possess. All of us can be leaders, and Eleanor's life proves that no obstacle is too great to stand in the way of realizing your own ability to lead. But the first step toward leadership is taking personal responsibility. If Eleanor's life held a central theme it is this: We are personally responsible for who we become, who we choose to be.

If Eleanor were here she would say, as she did to the women of her time, "Today is a challenge for women . . . tomorrow will see how [you] answer the challenge!"

CHAPTER ONE

Learn from
Your Past

*"Character building begins
in our infancy, and continues
until death."*

—ER

*I*n late 1933, at the end of her first year as first lady, Eleanor Roosevelt called her publisher to ask how her book, *It's Up to the Women*, was doing. The book had been published only a few months earlier, and Eleanor was anxious to learn how the public was responding to it. She was relieved to hear it was selling "very steadily."

Eleanor had written the book as a combination of homemaking advice and political manifesto. In a chapter called "The Problems of the Young Married," she counseled couples to show "an immense amount of tolerance and of unselfishness" toward each other. But being tolerant and unselfish didn't mean women must forgo all personal goals and ambitions. Women should also feel free to marry and have careers, she argued in a later chapter. "Women's lives must be adjusted and arranged for in just the same way that men's lives are," Eleanor wrote.

Eleanor had written her first book in the middle of a year when she also determinedly rewrote the role of first lady. She held the first-ever press conference by a president's wife and, to counter the all-male White House press corps, she admitted only women. She put together a team of women to work on getting women appointed to government jobs, an effort that resulted in Frances Perkins' appointment as FDR's secretary of labor, making her the first-ever woman cabinet member.

By August of 1933, Eleanor's leadership had begun to attract notice. Suffragist and political strategist Carrie Chapman Catt had pictures of statesmen hanging on her wall, "but under the new administration," she wrote to Eleanor, "I have been obliged to start a new collection, and that is one of stateswomen...and you are the very center of it all."

It's Up to the Women was part of a larger agenda. According to biographer Blanche Wiesen Cook, Eleanor wanted "to create a grassroots movement, led and informed by women," to carry out the social reforms of the New Deal. Her book stood like a banner in that effort. The small volume held a message that rested on foundations forged in Eleanor's childhood, especially the idea of personal responsibility and duty. She had taken these first leadership lessons, as many leaders do, from early experience. Just as *It's Up to the Women* called on women to make change, it had been up to Eleanor, as a child, to triumph over more misfortune than any child should have to face. But triumph she did, with the firm belief that if *she* could, anyone could.

Reflecting on her early life, Eleanor concluded that "one can, even without any particular gifts, overcome obstacles that seem insurmountable if one is willing to face the fact that they must be overcome; that, in spite of timidity and fear, in spite of a lack of special talents, one can find a way to live widely and fully."

She held to a simple understanding drawn from her childhood—you don't have to be special to lead a special life. That belief cemented her many and varied relationships. Eleanor had drawn a key lesson from her history and gained faith not only in her own ability but also in the ability of other people. Publishing *It's Up to the Women* was only one act of many that Eleanor took to inspire women by speaking to them as fellow travelers on the road to a better world.

In *Leadership: The Journey Inward*, Delorese Ambrose writes that self-knowledge is a prerequisite for leadership. Ambrose writes: "To transform our organizations, our communities, or our lives, we must first transform ourselves. Leadership development, then, becomes a process of self-reflection aimed at personal growth: a journey inward." It is a lifetime journey, one that begins by examining our childhood and determining the sources of our leadership.

First Understand Your Needs

On October 11, 1884, Eleanor was born into a family stricken by two deaths that had occurred on the same day earlier in the year. Her father, Elliott, had lost his mother on a foggy February night. Hours later, in the same house, his sister-in-law, Theodore's wife, died in childbirth.

"I must have been a more wrinkled and less attractive baby than the average," Eleanor wrote, "but to my father I was a miracle from Heaven." But Elliott's joy was crippled by grief over his mother's death. Before Eleanor's birth he had started leaving his household to drown himself in drink. His wife, Anna, young, pregnant, and abandoned, had little idea of what to do. Those who loved Elliott felt a "harrowing anxiety," in Eleanor's words. The charming, handsome man who had wooed the elegant Anna Hall had become an unpredictable alcoholic.

According to Eleanor, Anna was "one of the most beautiful women I have ever seen." High society agreed that Eleanor's mother had the frail, fair beauty and the proud, straight-backed bearing that made her the envy of her friends. As Eleanor grew, her lackluster looks and personality were hard for Anna to bear.

Anna's coldness contrasted with Elliott's adoring attentions to Eleanor, at least in his lucid moments. He showed Eleanor off to friends, asking her to dress up and dance for them. When she had finished he would swing her into the air as his friends' applause echoed in her ears. Good times with her father were exquisite for the little girl. She adored being allowed to watch him in his dressing room. She followed his preparations eagerly, always feeling "perfectly happy" when she was with him. In her autobiography, *This Is My Story*, she wrote of her father, "He dominated my life as long as he lived, and was the love of my life for many years after he died."

When Eleanor was two years old, the family visited James Roosevelt's elegant estate on the Hudson River in Hyde Park. Elliott had been named as a godparent to James Roosevelt's son, Franklin Delano, born two years before Eleanor. The children were fifth cousins once removed. At that first meeting between the future president and his future wife, Franklin, on all fours, bore Eleanor on his back around the nursery.

This story became part of family lore, and Eleanor recalled it years later. But another part of the story was less charming. At teatime, Eleanor stood in a starched white frock outside the library door, too shy to go in. Her mother called to her, "Come in, Granny," stinging the little girl's pride with derision that would be repeated as Eleanor grew. This despised description became incorporated into Eleanor's views of herself. "I was a solemn child," she wrote in her autobiography, "without beauty and painfully shy and I seemed like a little old woman entirely lacking in the spontaneous joy and mirth of youth."

Over the course of Eleanor's first eight years, Elliott's roller coaster behavior took the family across the globe searching for a cure for his addictions. But during their travels nothing seemed to work as planned. On their first trip abroad, when Eleanor was two and a half years old, the family crossed the Atlantic on the ship *Brittanic*. Only a day out of port, a steamer rammed the ship, sending passengers into screaming chaos. Hundreds of people were injured. In the horrific scene a child had an arm ripped off; another was beheaded. Elliott helped lower his wife, along with her sister and the baby nurse, into the quickly filling lifeboats. He jumped in and called to the seaman holding little Eleanor to drop her down to the boat. Elliott held his arms out to catch his daughter, but Eleanor clung in shrieking desperation to the man. Finally, prying her fingers loose, he dropped her safely into her father's arms.

The family returned immediately to New York, but after only a few days Eleanor's parents left again, intending to spend six months in Europe so Elliott might regain his health. Eleanor's parents chose to leave her behind with a great-aunt because she had become terrified of the water. But Eleanor felt that her parents had abandoned her because she hadn't acted more bravely on the *Brittanic*. After they had gone, she wondered aloud, "Where is baby's home now?"

Eleanor's question became a theme of her young life. By her fifth birthday little brother Elliott Jr. had been born, followed two years later by another brother. But her father's depression had deepened, and his brother, Theodore, insisted he leave the family. Theodore sent Elliott first to a treatment center for alcoholics, then to work in southern Virginia. Visits to his family were discouraged while he tried to get his life together and overcome his addictions.

Eleanor entered a dream-world built from promises her father made. They would be together one day. They would travel to wonderful places. She rushed to the door when the postman came, hoping for a letter. Eleanor's longing for her father was intensified by Anna's coldness to her daughter. Eleanor remembered standing in the doorway, her finger defiantly stuck in her mouth, watching her mother's attentions to her two brothers. "I felt a curious barrier between myself and these three," she wrote later. The loneliness and longing she felt soon turned to tragedy.

Barely two years after Elliott's exile from his family, Eleanor's home life was shattered again. Anna became ill, rapidly losing her strength. She died of diphtheria on December 7, 1892. Elliott wrote pleading letters from Abingdon, Virginia, begging to be allowed to see his wife as she lay sick. By the time Elliott arrived from Virginia, it was too late to say goodbye. "I can remember standing by a window," Eleanor wrote, "when Cousin Susie told me that my mother was dead.... Death meant nothing to me, and one fact wiped out everything else. My father was back and I would see him soon."

The children went to live with Anna's mother, who owned a grand but gloomy brownstone in Manhattan and a sprawling estate on the Hudson River at Tivoli, New York. During the children's stay at their grandmother's, Elliott's visits were erratic. Then, six months after Anna's death, Elliott suffered a final emotional blow. Four-year-old Elliott Jr. died from scarlet fever and diphtheria. Elliott's depression and his use of alcohol and drugs spiraled out of control. Fifteen months later, on August 14, 1894, Eleanor's beloved father was dead. Just a few months shy of her tenth birthday, Eleanor was an orphan.

"I simply refused to believe it," Eleanor wrote, "and while I wept long and went to bed still weeping I finally went to sleep and began the next day living in my dream-world as usual.... I knew in my mind that my father was dead, and yet I lived with him more closely, probably, than I had when he was alive."

In her earliest years, Eleanor's basic biological needs were met, but her need for security was not. "I was an exceptionally timid child," she wrote in her later years, "afraid of the dark, afraid of mice, afraid of practically everything."

As a result of her own difficult childhood experiences, Eleanor possessed a unique empathy with the sufferings of others. She brought that empathy to her leadership during three of the most fearful times in American history: World War I, the Depression, and World War II. The child who overcame her fears became the woman who rallied fearful constituents through the power of a common bond. She realized as she grew older that "painfully, step by step, I learned to stare down each of my fears, conquer it, attain the hard-earned courage to go on to the next. Only then was I really free."

Similarly, Eleanor's needs for affection and belonging were not met as a child. "There were things I wanted so much," Eleanor wrote, "things like love and affection." Yet this emotional deprivation seemed to become a leadership strength for Eleanor. She turned childhood craving for affection into a positive quest for attention and affection as a leader. James MacGregor Burns, a Pulitzer Prize-winning FDR biographer and leadership scholar, confirms this idea. "The need for affection and belongingness...has long been considered a stimulus toward political participation and leadership," says Burns.

Once Eleanor became active in public life, her leadership revolved around building larger and larger circles of followers and collaborators. She joined countless organizations, multiplying her ability to influence others, find allies, and take leadership. As first lady she traveled to meet housewives, farm families, miners, and workers of every ethnicity. She thrived on these relationships, and because of her genuine empathy for the suffering of others, she received overwhelming affection and acceptance.

Eleanor's childhood provides a model of how leadership grows from the needs of childhood. Your own life history will include a unique set of experiences related to your needs and their fulfillment. By reflecting on those experiences you can better understand what motivates you as a leader, and you can discover new ways to strengthen your leadership skills.

We Were All Followers Once

Children have no choice but to accept the leadership of their parents, or other legal guardians. Parents, as leaders in the context of family life, give us our first lessons in leadership.

We must follow them because they fulfill our physical needs, beginning with food, shelter, and other biological requirements. They also take care of our emotional needs, including security and love.

You can reframe your entire concept of leadership by looking at your childhood in a new way, as a series of leadership experiences. This gives you a new way to understand the source of your leadership inclinations, strengths, and challenges.

For instance, research suggests that being deprived of a physical need early in life can result in continuing problems with being a leader as well as a follower. People who carry the psychological weight of unfulfilled basic needs may find it difficult later in life to engage with the larger world. Their lingering preoccupation with ensuring the satisfaction of their basic needs can interfere with their ability to reach out and connect with other people, as leadership or followership requires.

The idea of thinking in terms of needs and fulfillment became the basis of a groundbreaking theory of psychologist Abraham Maslow, who suggested that there is a hierarchy of needs starting with the physiological. As needs are met at each level, higher needs emerge. After physiological needs are met, children have "safety" needs—the need for security and stability, for structure and freedom from fear or anxiety among others. After the safety needs, Maslow proposes that there is a need for love, affection, and belonging.

When these needs are met, the soil of our personality becomes a fertile environment for leadership to develop. However, the lack of one or more of these needs in our childhood doesn't mean we can't become leaders. In fact, deprivation may account for certain leadership drives. For example, Eleanor's tragic childhood became a source of leadership skills for her.

Search for Self-knowledge

Eleanor journeyed inward to develop her greatest leadership strength—her ability to connect with other people. Within herself she found the key that all leaders need: the ability to motivate other people, to move them toward an idea or vision.

"You must try to understand truthfully what makes you do things or feel things," Eleanor wrote. "Until you have been able to face the truth about yourself you cannot be really sympathetic or understanding in regard to what happens to other people."

Your memories, hopefully less traumatic than Eleanor's, are the starting point for understanding and using your leadership potential. The first step in learning leadership is learning about yourself as a leader through reflection on your life experiences. Leadership is a learning process. No gene has been isolated that makes some people leaders and others not. Leaders aren't born; they are made.

How do you start mobilizing your personal legacy as a leader? Ask yourself questions. What formative experiences can you remember? Don't confine yourself to your home life. What about school? Your social group? Events in your community, the country, and the world? Who were the most important people in your young life? What did they expect from you? What were their values? Sometimes thinking about the "sayings" in your household reveals this. For instance, I had an older brother who often played games such as chess, monopoly, or cards with me. Being older, he usually won. When I came close to winning, he liked to tease me by saying, "Almost isn't good enough." I've gained a better understanding of my competitive spirit and ambition from recognizing the effects of that taunt during my formative years. When something is really important (and beating my brother when I was nine years old was really important), I don't settle for almost succeeding.

One way to begin a reflection on your life is to write an autobiography of your childhood. Don't worry, no one but you ever has to see it. The act of writing down your thoughts and memories, however briefly you examine them, will bring out more thoughts and allow deeper reflection. If you think you don't have time, consider what Eleanor did.

In 1936, Eleanor began the first of the three volumes of her autobiography. By that time she had been first lady for three years, and her life was bursting with activities, from lectures to White House duties to her continuing work to push New Deal programs for social reform to dealing with the ups and downs of five grown children. Yet she insisted on writing every word of her autobiography herself, and in the process, she learned about the act of reflection.

Eleanor shared her insight with a farm woman whom she had encouraged to write about her own life. "Block out your early youth," Eleanor wrote to Alma W. Johnson of Rogers, Arkansas. "Start with your very first memory, putting in as many incidents as possible which will show up your relationship to your parents, the effect of circumstances upon you, the things you learned and the way your character was formed by the circumstances of your life, and the influence, conscious or unconscious, of your parents."

As you take time to know yourself, take Eleanor's advice for uncovering your memories and understanding their impact on your leadership abilities. Remember that "even in the childhood years," as Burns writes, "the road toward leadership roles takes some form and direction."

Anne M. Mulcahy, chief executive of the Xerox Corporation, acknowledged this idea in an article in the *Wall Street Journal* in 2001. She described a "gender-neutral household" where her mother provided a powerful role model who acted as an equal with Mulcahy's father. "Seeing how influential she was helped me immeasurably in developing my own independence." Heated dinner table debates with her parents and four brothers led Mulcahy to find her authenticity as a leader. "I have expected to be defined by—

and succeed because of—values, character, and intellect," Mulcahy says.

Like Eleanor and Anne Mulcahy, you can discover clues to your leadership development by exploring your childhood.

Spin Bad Memories into Leadership Strengths

Before his death, Eleanor's father, however erratic, was virtually the only source of nurturing and love for his daughter. He dominated Eleanor's thoughts. When she heard him come in the house, she "slid down the banisters and usually catapulted into his arms before his hat was hung up." Elliott encouraged Eleanor to study, to be disciplined. Anna, on the other hand, simply hoped Eleanor would learn good manners to make up for her lack of beauty. Eleanor felt she was always disgracing her mother—by throwing tantrums, by eating sweets when they were forbidden, or by being too shy to answer questions. Even the French nanny who tended to Eleanor tormented her with small cruelties, such as pulling her hair. Eleanor's self-image teetered on the edge of collapse. But she rallied herself through imagination.

After her father's death, Eleanor and her brother continued living with Grandmother Hall. Eleanor's grandmother developed a strict host of rules for Eleanor. For example, Eleanor had to read special books on Sunday. She had to pray at the start and end of every day. Scratchy flannels were practically a uniform she wore from November to April, and cold sponge baths were a daily routine. Catching colds or having headaches were Eleanor's fault, and her grandmother considered them "foolishness." And reading in bed before breakfast was strictly forbidden.

In the great high-ceilinged house at Tivoli, Eleanor spent her hours alone with books from the family library. She wandered into the woods and fields, losing herself in reading. And whenever she could, she escaped into her elaborate fantasy life with her father.

"This power of imagination is a kind of defense in childhood," Eleanor admitted. But she also saw the positive role that developing an active imagination had had on her adult life. "If used correctly, [imagination] makes it more possible for you later on to imagine what other people are like and what they think and feel. It helps to keep you curious, anxious to understand what is going on around you . . . . If it is nourished and directed, it can become a flame that lights the way to new things, new ideas, new experience."

Eleanor's positive view of otherwise painful memories is typical of her analysis of her childhood. Because she believed that "one's childhood marked one's future life," she also had to develop an optimistic assessment of her past. Without this positive spin she might have collapsed under the weight of the tragedies of her youth.

Eleanor proves that it's possible to be a product of your past, but not its victim. As the saying goes, "It's never too late to have a happy childhood." Eleanor's leadership grew from her acceptance of her past and her understanding of how she had transformed herself through it. "I think somehow we learn who we really are," she said, "and then live with that decision."

To use the experience of your past to develop your leadership, focus—as Eleanor did—on the benefits that you can draw from early experiences. That's easy to do when your memories are positive.

Marita Fegley, communications director for the national tax division of the professional services firm Ernst and Young, has great memories of learning loyalty and teamwork as a child. When Fegley was nine years old, she tried out for the all-boys soccer team. Not only did she make it, she became an outstanding player. "I learned what loyalty meant on that team. When we played other teams the boys would try to pick on me because I was the only girl. But my teammates were fierce in defending me on the field." Fegley also learned about teamwork. "I was taught that if I scored I had to point to the person who assisted. And my parents reinforced values of character over winning at all costs. Now my colleagues admire my ability to give other people credit and to work collaboratively."

Whether your childhood experiences are mostly painful like Eleanor's, or mostly joyful like Marita Fegley's or, more likely, somewhere in between, you need to draw the positive life lessons from those experiences. This is the beginning of a lifelong process of holding a mirror to your inner self to bring effective leadership to your life's work.

John W. Gardner, author of *On Leadership* and founder of Common Cause, writes, "In leadership at its finest, the leader symbolizes the best in the community, the best in its traditions, values, and purposes." Eleanor exemplified leadership at its finest, but she achieved that status by starting with herself, looking inward with honesty and curiosity. This enabled her to change the world around her. "In her personal struggle for self-awareness," wrote a British social critic, "she was the greatest of the Roosevelts."

$\mathscr{E}$LEANOR'S WAY

- Your childhood is a leadership legacy. Reflect on it and use it to build your leadership.

- Be honest with yourself as you think back to your earliest memories.

- Be as curious about exploring your memories as you are about making new discoveries.

- Think anecdotally; try to remember actual events that lead to broader memories.

- Connect your memories to your leadership goals and values.

- Explore the meaning of family traditions and sayings and how they contribute to your leadership traits.

- Consider writing an "autobiography" as a way of examining your past.

- Reflect on your past and connect it with new experience.

- As you draw on your memories, focus on the positive lessons that can help you reach your goals.

CHAPTER TWO

Find Mentors
and Advisers

"All my life I have been grateful for her [Mlle. Souvestre's] influence."
—ER

*I*n the summer of 1899, Eleanor, fifteen years old and nearly six feet tall, walked with well-rehearsed posture and grace into her grandmother's study. Grandmother Hall had big news. "Your mother wanted you to go to boarding school in Europe," she told Eleanor, "and I have decided to send you, child." The school could only be Allenswood in England, where Eleanor adored Auntie Bye had been educated. Years before, Eleanor's parents had met and liked Allenswood's headmistress, Mademoiselle Marie Souvestre. "Thus," remembered Eleanor, "the second period of my life began."

Eleanor sailed across the Atlantic with her Aunt Tissie. Following the older woman's lead, Eleanor hardly left her cabin. By the time they docked, she walked ashore as if emerging from a cocoon, shaky and unsure of her first steps. When her aunt left her at her new school, Eleanor remembered feeling "lost and very lonely." This changed when Eleanor came to know Mlle. Souvestre.

To Eleanor, Mlle. Souvestre, whom she nicknamed "Sou," was "far and away the most impressive and fascinating person" at the Allenswood School. Eleanor described the seventy-year-old headmistress as "short and rather stout, [with] snow-white hair. Her head was beautiful, with clear-cut, strong features, a very strong face and broad forehead. Her hair grew to a peak in front and waved back in natural waves to a twist at the back of her head. Her eyes looked through you, and she always knew more than she was told."

The Allenswood School was housed in a rambling Tudor mansion with many gables and tall bay windows, in a little town called South Fields. About thirty girls were living and studying there when Eleanor arrived. Having had a French nurse, Eleanor fit in easily at the French-speaking school and quickly became one of Mlle. Souvestre's favorites.

Eleanor's compassionate and empathetic nature, likely a result of her childhood traumas, made her a powerful influence on the other girls. She readily helped the less able students. She gravitated to those who needed a friend. Eleanor's schoolmates showed their affection for her on Saturdays when, according to custom, flowers or books were left in the rooms of girls who were most admired. Violets filled Eleanor's room each week.

Eleanor's effect on others quickly became apparent to everyone, including the headmistress. In a note to Eleanor's grandmother, Souvestre praised "the purity of [Eleanor's] heart, the nobleness of her thought . . . verified by her conduct among people who were at first perfect strangers to her." Souvestre delighted in Eleanor's interest "in everything she comes in contact with," and she cultivated that interest.

Although Eleanor had always been an eager learner, she had been taught that curiosity was a fault. That changed one evening when Eleanor and the other girls gathered in Souvestre's library. Souvestre said, "You must cultivate curiosity, for only through curiosity can you learn, not only what there is in books, but what lies around you in the world of things and people." With this, Eleanor felt she had been freed to follow her natural inclination to learn about everyone and everything. Souvestre became her guide, and "day by day," Eleanor wrote, "I found myself more interested in her."

Eleanor had found a great mentor. Throughout her life, Mlle. Souvestre's influence would guide her, and it would encourage her openness to other mentors in later years.

As we develop leadership skills, we all need mentors to guide and support us. "Nobody makes it without a mentor," says Sheila Wellington, president of Catalyst, a group that works to advance women in business, and author of *Become Your Own Mentor*. In a Catalyst study entitled "Women of Color Executives: Their Voices, Their Journeys," Wellington identifies mentoring as a key to success. "Lack of mentors was cited by women of color as the biggest barrier to success . . . . Despite exclusionary cultures, these women found and developed mentoring relationships with influential people in their organizations. They knew how critical to their success it was and they figured out a way to make it happen."

As Karin Klenke discusses in *Women and Leadership*, mentoring is a way for all women to break through the glass ceilings that get in the way of women's success and leadership.

Mentoring gives women the tools to overcome negative leadership stereotypes because mentors "act as transfer agents of organizational leadership." They can provide both visibility within the organization and strategies for working the system.

You need to remember the importance of finding your own Mlle. Souvestre, not once, but many times as you move forward as a leader. For you, as for Eleanor, mentors will help you take leadership to a new level, opening new possibilities and creating greater opportunities. As Eleanor wrote, "What you are in life results in great part from the influence exerted on you over the years by just a few people."

Good Mentors Are Hard to Find— But Don't Give Up

Eleanor was lucky to have had Mlle. Souvestre's guidance. The headmistress's mission was to help her students become strong leaders. She taught them to be independent of mind and spirit, socially responsible, intellectually and personally courageous. Those girls who won her special attention, as Eleanor did, received regular doses of her philosophy. Eleanor's biographer, Blanche Wiesen Cook, writes Souvestre was "a passionate humanist committed to social justice, [who] inspired young women to think about leadership, to think for themselves, and above all to think about a nobler, more decent future."

Like most women, it's unlikely you'll be lucky enough to be placed on the doorstep of a brilliant teacher, eager to step into the role of mentor. Instead, you will have to actively seek a role model who can teach you the unspoken rules, give you advice, and foster your leadership qualities and growth.

The workplace barriers women face can make it difficult to find a mentor. Traditional mentoring relationships often involve an older and more savvy professional and a younger protégé, and women may be intimidated about asking successful veterans for their guidance. Further, the relative shortage of women in leadership may make it more difficult to find a woman mentor. And sometimes successful women are hesitant to become mentors because the potential failure of their protégé tends to reflect more negatively on them than on a man, or because they may be worried about seeming to "favor" other women by mentoring them.

Although women can also seek out and benefit from a male mentor, gender barriers can get in the way. Klenke discusses research showing that male mentors had less confidence in women as managers and were reluctant to take on women as protégés until the women "had proven themselves." In addition, women as well as potential male mentors may fear sparking rumors of an improper workplace relationship.

There are many reasons why women have difficulty cultivating a relationship with a mentor, but finding mentors is an important element in building personal leadership skills, especially for women. Amy Handlin makes this point in her book, *Whatever Happened to the Year of the Woman?* According to Handlin, one of the conditions that keeps women from advancing in corporations is "an absence of mentoring opportunities . . . . Male managers tend to have informal networks that provide contacts, feedback, and career guidance. Excluded from these 'old boy networks,' women need mentors to provide alternative sources of support."

It's essential that you seek out mentors for yourself. Of course, you don't have to say "Will you be my mentor?" although some women have done just that. You can begin by finding the chance to talk with someone you respect and whom you believe can be helpful, or you can ask for a time to meet. In seeking out a mentor, don't be afraid to show your enthusiasm. People are more interested in helping people who seem likely to take and use the advice offered. Work in stages so you have time to assess if the person will be helpful, and so he or she will have a reasonable opportunity to get to know you. Ask about the person's experiences and talk about your own. Be direct in asking questions. Finally, assume the person will be flattered and open to helping you; however, if that's not the case, ask for suggestions for others who can offer guidance.

I found my first career mentor when I lived in Albany, New York, in the early 1970s. I had dropped out of college and was working in a dead-end clerical job. With more than a casual interest in women and low-wage work, I had volunteered to get a speaker for a local women's group. I invited Anne Nelson, who ran a program for women involved in unions as part of Cornell University's School of Industrial and Labor Relations.

Besides giving a wonderful talk, Anne stayed at my house for the night. I was in awe of this very accomplished woman who had started a unique and powerful center at the university, and I was excited about the opportunity to talk with her one-on-one. Anne counseled me about the importance of finishing school and emphasized how much the labor movement needed women leaders. She suggested I enroll in Cornell's labor studies program in Albany, and I followed her advice. Anne and I kept in touch, and a short time after our first meeting, she received funding for a program to help women state workers, and she hired me as her assistant. With Anne's guidance I finished my degree, went on to law school, and enjoyed a two-decade long career in the labor movement.

Although mentoring relationships are often formed in the workplace, sometimes as part of an organizational plan, the office is not the only place to find a mentor. The best mentor for you may be in the ranks of a rival business, on the exercise machine next to you at the gym, or among relatives or friends.

Remember that mentors can be both formal or informal, short-term and long-term. During my time in Albany I formed a brief mentoring relationship with a much older woman who was chief-of-staff to the lieutenant governor. Despite our short acquaintance, she gave me one of the best pieces of advice I've ever received. "Don't make the mistake I did," she once told me. "When I was younger, I knew I should have left my job and I didn't. I stayed way too long and missed some great opportunities. If it's time to move on, then move on." I took her advice to heart when I made the difficult decision to leave my job at Cornell to get a law degree, and again fifteen years later when I left my lobbying job to become a writer.

As you keep your eye out for mentors, ask, "Who can help me with the decisions that will shape my life and leadership abilities today?" "Who can help me learn what I need to move toward my goals?" "Whom do I admire, and who's doing what I'd like to be doing?" These questions are particularly important when you're "stuck" and need advice to help you progress. In fact the word "mentor" came from just such a situation, which arose in Homer's classic narrative, *The Odyssey*.

In Homer's tale, the goddess Athena took the form of an experienced and trusted Ithacan counselor named Mentor. She advised Odysseus's son, Telemachus, to stop sitting around waiting for his father and instead sail off to find him. As Karin Klenke notes in *Women and Leadership*, "Like all good mentors, Athena imbued Telemachus with a sense of courage and morality and set him off on a journey to explore his leadership potential."

Believe that your Mentor is out there waiting to help. With focus and persistence, you will find her and others who will help you develop as a leader.

Good Mentors Touch Your Life— Not Just Your Career

Marie Souvestre's influence touched all aspects of Eleanor's life. Intellectually, the headmistress demanded the greatest rigor. Eleanor loved the history class Souvestre taught and did well in it. She recalled the treatment reserved for girls who didn't meet the teacher's standard. "I have seen [Souvestre] take a girl's paper and tear it in half in her disgust and anger at poor or shoddy work."

Occasionally, Eleanor and a few other girls were invited to Souvestre's study in the evening. These were Eleanor's "red-letter days." She remembered Souvestre having "a great gift for reading aloud and she read to us, always in French, poems, plays, or stories. If the poems were those she liked, occasionally she read them over two or three times, and then demanded that we recite them to her in turn." Where other girls went mute with anxiety, Eleanor found this challenge "exhilarating."

At Allenswood, Eleanor also became physically renewed. The headaches that had plagued her in her grandmother's cheerless, tense household disappeared. Her appetite grew. She tried team sports and made the first team in field hockey. "I think that day was one of the proudest moments of my life," she later recalled. Unlike many of the other girls who suffered from sores on their hands or feet from the icy cold within Allenswood's walls, Eleanor strode outside for daily walks unbothered. "I never spent healthier years. I cannot remember being ill for a day." She found emotional release as well, feeling secure enough to cry publicly, to have her first temper tantrum, and to gain internal strength. "For the first time in all my life," she wrote, "all my fears left me."

During the Christmas break of 1899, Souvestre took Eleanor with her to Paris. Once there, she told Eleanor that her clothes were outdated and unflattering. At sixteen, Eleanor still followed fashion rules imposed by her grandmother and wore dresses that belonged on a child. Eleanor jumped at the chance to spend her allowance for a new dress. "I still remember my joy in that dark red dress, made for me by a small dressmaker in Paris . . . it had all the glamour of being my first French dress. I wore it on Sundays and as an everyday evening dress at school and probably got more satisfaction out of it than from any dress I have had since!"

The best mentors are those who, like Mlle. Souvestre, touch us beyond our practical needs. They do more than explain the politics behind a management decision or suggest where to look for the next step up the company ladder. In discussions with women about political careers, author Amy Handlin discovered that although women were looking for mentors who could be helpful professionally and politically, they also hoped for a mentor who could give personal guidance in terms of everything from emotional issues to dress and deportment. Research shows that the best mentors provide career progress as well as social and emotional support.

The mentors you choose should help you navigate the unspoken rules of the organization—that is, they should teach you about office politics. They should be savvy analysts of organizational culture and personalities. They must be willing to bring you into their networks, and help you move up the organizational ladder. Finally, they must be willing to give you honest and effective criticism.

Great mentors are the people who see deeper into your heart than you can see yourself. They have the nature of the best teachers, patient and loving, and the wisdom to give you the advice that you need when you are ready to receive it. They take a deep interest in you because giving others the benefit of their knowledge and insight gives them satisfaction and fulfillment. They are unselfish with their time and advice, but not without the ego that drives their desire to see you succeed or the desire to be rewarded for spotting new talent. If you find such a mentor, she or he will not only lead you on your future professional path but also help you to realize your full potential—spiritually, mentally, and emotionally.

Be Open to Your Mentors as They Open You to New Ideas

Some of the greatest challenges Marie Souvestre posed to Eleanor's view of the world came when they traveled together. These times were to Eleanor "the most momentous things that happened in my education . . . a revelation. [Souvestre] did all the things that in a vague way you had always felt you wanted to do."

On a train ride along the Mediterranean coast, her mentor touched Eleanor's passion for a world open to spontaneity and the whims of a restless heart. The duo was traveling to the famous town of Pisa, passing by a lovely seaside town. As Eleanor told the story, "the guard called out 'Alassio.' Mlle. Souvestre was galvanized into action; breathlessly she leaned out of the window and said, 'I am going to get off.' Directing me to get the bags, which were stored on the rack over our heads, we simply fell off onto the platform, bag and baggage, just before the train started on its way. I was aghast." Eleanor had traveled with her grandmother from New York to Tivoli many times, and Grandmother Hall wouldn't have dreamed of altering her carefully arranged plans. But Souvestre told Eleanor that she had a friend living in Alassio. More important, she wanted to watch the stars come out in sight of the lovely blue of the Mediterranean. Eleanor felt a thrill. "Never again would I be the rigid little person I had been theretofore."

Perhaps more important, Souvestre taught Eleanor true independence. While Grandmother Hall considered an unchaperoned young woman a scandal, Souvestre let Eleanor wander the streets of Florence with nothing but a map and her wits. Because she was elderly, Souvestre put the sixteen-year-old to work packing and unpacking, looking up trains, getting tickets, making detailed arrangements, all the while building Eleanor's self-confidence and practical knowledge.

Mlle. Souvestre did have a dramatic effect on Eleanor, but she wouldn't be her last mentor. Eleanor's roles changed over the decades, and she found new mentors along the way. Similarly, if you find yourself facing new challenges at any point in your life, remember that your leadership will best be served by finding one or more new mentors for guidance. Eleanor did just that nearly two decades after she left the loving guidance of Marie Souvestre.

In 1920, when Eleanor was entering her late thirties, Louis Howe, Franklin Roosevelt's close political confidant, advised her in developing her natural gifts for communication and politics. Howe and FDR wanted Eleanor to help her husband politically by giving speeches and stumping on the campaign trail during FDR's run for vice-president. She was sure that she would fail. But Eleanor recalled a conversation with Howe that began a close and powerful mentorship. "You can do anything you have to do," Howe said firmly. "Get out and try." He proceeded to help Eleanor develop relationships with the press and to become an effective public speaker. With Howe's help Eleanor learned to become a leader who could communicate her ideas for social change with powerful results.

It does little good to find great mentors if you're unwilling to follow their advice. It's a mentor's job to challenge you to grow and change, to tell you things you may not want to hear. A mentor who is unable to do that wouldn't be very valuable to you. Like Eleanor, you must be ready to open yourself to a mentoring experience, and recognize that your strength as a leader will grow and change as a result.

Mentoring Is a Reciprocal Relationship

Louis Howe's efforts for Eleanor, like those of Souvestre, were rewarded by another phenomenon of mentoring—reciprocal experience. The mentoring relationship is never one way, although the crosscurrents may be subtle. Howe, one of the best behind-the-scenes political operatives of his time, got enormous satisfaction from Eleanor's increasing influence. He even wanted her to run for president and encouraged her in that direction.

Mlle. Souvestre's letters similarly reveal a mentor who had gained as much from the relationship as she had given. In the summer of 1902, Eleanor had been forced to sail back to New York on her grandmother's command. "Mlle. Souvestre had become one of the people whom I cared most for in the world," Eleanor wrote. "I would have given a great deal to have spent another year on my education, but to my grandmother the age of eighteen was the time that you 'came out,' and not to 'come out' was unthinkable."

A few months after Eleanor left Allenswood, Souvestre wrote to her, "I would like to have you with me. I miss you every day of my life." Later, when the new school year started, the headmistress wrote, "Ah! How we miss you here, my dear child. There are many new girls and, as is their habit, the English girls do not know how to welcome them, and leave them in the corner. You would have known how to make them feel rapidly at ease, and happy in circumstances so different from their usual lives . . . ." Eleanor and her mentor kept up their correspondence, but Eleanor never saw Marie Souvestre again. The great woman died two weeks after Eleanor's marriage in March 1905.

Souvestre had helped Eleanor develop her leadership abilities, and Eleanor had used her newly developed skills to help her mentor, teacher, and friend. Every positive mentoring relationship has some element of reciprocal experience. Older mentors often benefit by gaining insight into a younger generation's culture. Further, today's rapid transitions to new levels of technology mean younger people, who are closer to school-based learning, can help older mentors discover useful innovations. And mentorships can turn into friendships when those who were mentored take their place in leadership and the exchange becomes more equal. This was true for Elizabeth McNulty, vice president of creative design for a well-known clothing company.

McNulty's position gives her the chance to hire many young designers looking for opportunities to advance. "I always prefer to hire young people with little experience versus the over-experienced." McNulty explains that "the challenge is to teach others and advance others through my personal experience. My theory is that you're hiring your replacement. They should be able to do everything I can do. I don't want to hold onto information, like some people do thinking they're protecting their jobs. By really mentoring people I can have the freedom to look upward to my boss and learn more myself, or take an opportunity to advance."

A few years ago McNulty hired Suzanne Morse, a young woman straight from college. McNulty and Morse only worked together for six months, but McNulty recognized Morse's creativity and ambition, and they liked each other. Three years later, when McNulty got the opportunity to start a home-products line at her company, she called McNulty to work with her. "I knew she would be perfect," McNulty explained. "I showed her how to turn her thoughts and creativity into reality through manufacturing. She had the enthusiasm to take advantage when I included her in everything and showed her everything. I took her to meetings, explained the politics of the corporate environment, and we succeeded together."

After two years Morse got a great offer—the chance to launch a home-products line at another company. "I'm glad she had the chance to be a leader somewhere else," McNulty said, "but we still seek each other's advice and we're friends. Helping a young person like her succeed made me feel that I accomplished something. And I think I instilled the desire to be a mentor in her." McNulty calls the relationship "a great success story of mentoring, being a mentor and also becoming friends along the way."

The continued relationships and loyalty that grow from a positive mentoring experience can have benefits far in the future, as both parties continue their careers. In *The Connective Edge*, Jean Lipmen-Blumen writes, "Protégés contribute to their mentors' continuing success by keeping them informed about important new events, by protecting the mentor's reputation and fortunes, and by alerting the mentor to new professional developments."

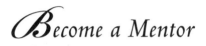ecome a Mentor

The reciprocal benefits of mentoring are one reason to consider being a mentor. You can also expect a great deal of satisfaction from seeing someone succeed thanks, in part, to your efforts. Recognizing the far-reaching benefits of mentoring, more and more companies are setting up mentoring programs that institutionalize these relationships and reward leaders for stepping forward and helping individuals coming up in the organization. Business and women's associations also offer mentoring networks, and can be good places to share what you know with a protégé.

It is particularly important for women to act as mentors for other women. Because there are far too few public models of women leaders—from politics to Fortune 500 companies—young women don't see the public face of women in leadership. By stepping forward as mentors, women leaders can help remedy this imbalance.

As she grew into the most recognized woman leader in the country, Eleanor also grew as a mentor to women throughout America. She wrote that for years she had been receiving "letters from all sorts of persons living in every part of our country. Always I have wished that I could reach these correspondents and many more with messages which perhaps might help them . . . ." To achieve that goal, Eleanor started a column in the *Woman's Home Companion* in 1933 and titled her first piece "I Want You to Write to Me." Hundreds of thousands did.

In that first article, Eleanor cautioned her readers that she wasn't infallible and wouldn't know all the answers. But it may be, she wrote, "that in the varied life I have had there have been certain experiences which other people will find useful . . . ." For the rest of her life, Eleanor offered her advice in thousands of letters, in books and articles, and in personal contact that changed many lives.

She also kept Marie Souvestre's picture and letters with her, perhaps as a reminder of the importance not only of having a mentor but also of being a mentor. "Whatever I have become since," Eleanor wrote years later, "had its seeds in those three years of contact with a liberal mind and strong personality."

ℰLEANOR'S WAY

- ▓ Be proactive about finding mentors. Don't make excuses that stop you from pursuing opportunities.

- ▓ Recognize that you can't know everything. Look for a mentor who can help in your weaker areas or with new challenges.

- ▓ You have nothing to lose and everything to gain by seeking the advice of someone you respect and endeavoring to establish a long-term relationship for future guidance.

- ▓ Remember that mentors can give you guidance professionally as well as socially and emotionally.

- ▓ Be open and willing to learn from your mentor.

- ▓ Your mentor may be older or younger than you, at your job or in your family, better educated or not. Be flexible in finding the best mentor for your needs at any given time.

- ▓ You can have more than one mentor at a time and will likely have more than one mentor over the course of your career.

- ▓ Maintain strong social networks that complement your mentoring relationships and support you when you are not in a mentoring relationship.

■ Remember that mentoring is a reciprocal experience. Look for ways to use your growing leadership skills to help your mentor.

■ As you learn, grow, and change, as you become more secure and powerful in your ability to lead, look for opportunities to be a mentor.

CHAPTER THREE

Mothering: Training for Leadership

"Remember that a home requires all the tact and all the executive ability required in any business."

—ER

*E*leanor stepped carefully down the circular stairway, her court train trailing many steps behind. Her satin wedding gown, tailored to her slim waist, flowed under Grandmother Hall's rose-point Brussels lace—the same lace that had covered Eleanor's mother's wedding dress. The thick chestnut rolls of Eleanor's hair were swept under a veil, fastened by her mother's diamond crescent. A riot of lilies of the valley sprouted from her bouquet. It was the balmy late winter afternoon of March 17, 1905. Eleanor had chosen her mother's birthday to marry Franklin Delano Roosevelt.

The ceremony was held in a grand New York City townhouse belonging to one of Eleanor's cousins on her mother's side. The drawing room held more than two hundred guests. Eleanor entered the room on the arm of her Uncle Ted, president of the United States. Many guests thought, in this moment at least, that they saw the beautiful image of Anna in her daughter's face.

Eleanor had reconnected with her distant cousin Franklin after she returned from Allenswood School in London. A Harvard man, Franklin stood tall, slim, and patrician, full of confidence and quick to offer his engaging smile. He descended from the Hyde Park Roosevelts rather than from Eleanor's Oyster Bay clan. The only child of an adoring, domineering mother, Franklin was a godson of Eleanor's late father, Elliott. But no Roosevelt captured his admiration and imagination more than the man escorting his bride down the aisle—Teddy Roosevelt.

Franklin had courted many of the most beautiful girls in New York's high society. Although some in his set saw him as a lightweight, a bit of a priss, even a "mama's boy," he had enough personal depth, and perhaps some vision of his future, to see beyond Eleanor's less attractive features. Yes, her chin receded and her teeth were too prominent. ("Her mouth and teeth seem to have no future," her Aunt Edith wrote a friend.) Still, Eleanor's eyes were lively and warm, and her intelligence and maturity often earned her a seat next to the most prominent hosts. "Cousin Eleanor has a very good mind," Franklin told his mother. But Sara Roosevelt, Franklin's widowed mother, connived to thwart the romance. "You're too young to get married" was one of the many reasons she offered for putting off marriage plans. Eleanor privately thought that Sara wanted Franklin to make "a more worldly and social match." Sara insisted the engagement be kept secret for a year, at the end of which she reluctantly accepted her son's choice.

After the wedding and European honeymoon, the couple returned to a house Sara had rented and furnished for them, just three blocks away from her own residence. The older woman also had made sure that servants were in place for Eleanor and Franklin, leaving few decisions for Eleanor to make. Motivated by an almost desperate desire to please Franklin and his mother, and to fit in with the tight-knit Hyde Park clan, Eleanor donned the mantle of cooperative, sub-servient helpmate. As her friend and biographer Joseph Lash wrote, "In return for the privilege of loving and being loved she stifled any impulse to assert herself." As Eleanor later recalled, "I was beginning to be an entirely dependent person, no tickets to buy, no plans to make, someone always to decide everything for me . . . . I was fitting pretty well into the pattern of a fairly conventional, quiet, young society matron."

Not long after settling into her new home and new role as Franklin's wife, Eleanor discovered the source of the nausea that had been plaguing her. She was pregnant. On May 3, 1906, her only daughter was born. The next year Eleanor bore the first of her five sons, one of whom died in infancy. The task of mothering overwhelmed Eleanor. "I was completely unprepared to be a practical housekeeper, wife, or mother," she wrote. Sara seized on Eleanor's insecurity and took con-trol. She insisted on hiring nannies to handle the childrearing duties as was typical for the Roosevelt's social class, and the new mother agreed. Meanwhile, Franklin was busy pursuing his law career and watching for his first political opportunity.

Eleanor had become a wife and mother of her times. She found herself in a role that, as a person orphaned at a young age, she had little experience for. For the next ten years her life would revolve around husband and children, though

LEADERSHIP THE ELEANOR ROOSEVELT WAY

her children would later fault her parenting, and she faulted herself for not spending more time with them. Nevertheless, it was in the family context that Eleanor learned many leadership lessons. Her home life gave her the chance to test her ability to lead and her values, much like mothers today.

Today, there is a growing recognition that work and home-based skills and values are interdependent. In his best-selling book *The Fifth Discipline*, Peter Senge quotes Bill O'Brien, CEO of Hanover Insurance. "The more I understand the real skills of leadership in a learning organization, the more I become convinced that these are the skills of effective parenting." Senge goes on, "Leading in a learning organization involves supporting people in clarifying and pursuing their own vision, 'moral suasion,' helping people discover underlying causes of problems, and empowering them to make choices. What could be a better description of effective parenting?"

Senge is right. Rather than buy into notions that devalue motherhood or detach it from the larger world, you can embrace the idea of mothering as a powerful foundation for your leadership.

Mothering: A Metaphor for Leading

In the male vernacular, sports, gambling, and the military serve as metaphors for leadership. Achieving a goal is a "touchdown." Taking a risk is "shooting a three-pointer" or "rolling the dice." Directions for a task may be shortened to "you know the drill."

Women, especially in male-dominated organizations, often try to use male metaphors, but often it's not a comfortable fit. Most women don't equate leadership with the same kinds of activities as men do. The metaphor that women can most often equate with leadership is mothering, with family life as the model for organizational life and dynamics. This is true even for women who have no children, because all learned from their mothers and grew up with the potential to become mothers. Many women without children of their own become mothers suddenly as stepparents or as "mothers" to an elderly parent. Older siblings often become "little mothers." The caregiving role becomes central to women's view of leadership. It is a touchstone for understanding the behavior of others, for translating women's experience into new leadership roles, and for making sense of women's leadership actions.

This phenomenon became a surprise finding in a study called "Inside Women's Power: Learning from Leaders," published in 2001 by the Wellesley College Center for Research on Women. Sixty women leaders ranging in age from thirty to seventy were interviewed for the study, including CEOs, politicians, and well-known women such as authors Ellen Goodman and Maya Angelou and television correspondent Lesley Stahl. Co-author Sumru Ekrut found that these women were "secure enough in their leadership positions to bring language from their lived experience as women to describe what they do." Many of the women interviewed for the study used maternal and family roles to describe their leadership or the leadership of other women. One leader said that she leads "warmly, like a mom. I try to lead like a parent. And I'm proud of what I consider my woman-like characteristics. I'm warm, I'm very huggy. I have a sense of humor that lets me kind of fit . . . into very threatening subjects. I listen and listen and listen and listen."

Women of color interviewed for the Wellesley study were particularly attuned to the idea of mothering as a leadership metaphor. As other researchers have noted, in the African American community, motherhood is a "symbol of power" and the way to "uplift the race." The Wellesley study explains, "For leaders who are women of color, mothering metaphors for leadership allude to mothers' transformative power to bring people along."

You may feel that it's risky to use mothering as a metaphor for leadership in the workplace. After all, the culture honors the ideal of mothering but attaches no value to it in economic terms. This schizophrenic approach puts the idea of mothering on a pedestal of sand. When women who have stayed home with children are ready to reenter the workforce, they are counseled to ignore or downplay their roles as mothers and instead to talk about volunteer work or maybe a little consulting they did in their free time. The clear implication is that mothering holds no connection to leadership and management ability. Women who work part-time face a similar division of their lives—their role as mother-leaders is seen as irrelevant at best, or distracting at worst, from their role in the workplace.

Women are the primary caretakers of home and children whether they work or not. In her groundbreaking book, *The Price of Motherhood*, Ann Crittendon notes that mothers who work outside the home have "their principal place of business in the home." Crittendon convincingly makes the case for ending the cultural denial of mothering's importance as demonstrated by the lack of economic value attached to it. She argues that mothering should be fully recognized for its value to the economy and for the skills involved in its execution.

Eleanor would have appreciated that Crittendon starts out with a quote from Theodore Roosevelt: "The good mother, the wise mother . . . is more important to the community than even the ablest man; her career is more worthy of honor and is more useful to the community than the career of any man, no matter how successful." Crittendon goes on to argue that, in terms of wealth creation for the country, the "human capital" represented by mothering is the greatest engine for generating the wealth that we have. What could be more important for the continued strength and growth of the country than children raised with love, compassion, and attention to personal development? "Changing the status of mothers, by gaining real recognition for their work," she argues, "is the great unfinished business of the women's movement."

Crittendon has an ambitious list of changes that employers, the government, the community, and husbands can make to raise the status of mothering. But one immediate change that women have under their control is to incorporate the metaphor of mothering into their life outside the home and make it a powerful leadership platform.

Barbara Mossberg did just that when she applied for the job of president of Goddard College in Vermont. In answering the question, "What are the three most important accomplishments in your life?" Mossberg wrote, "I don't know if one's children can be seen as 'accomplishments,' but certainly I view creating a nurturing structure in which to witness and guide the growth of unique human beings my most important goal to achieve. I don't take credit for my children, but to me they feel like fabulous accomplishments of my life." Mossberg got the job, and the board was so impressed by her responses that they were posted on the college Web site.

Raising children is an accomplishment that takes leadership of the highest order, the kind that is built on treasured values. Whether you have children or not, whether you are in the paid workforce full time, part time, or not at all, as a woman you have unique experience with mothering as leadership. "The traditional ways of talking about leadership," write the authors of the Wellesley study, "mask the many strengths women bring to their successful lives as leaders." Free yourself to think and talk about leadership in ways that make sense to your life as a woman and as a mother.

Mothering Teaches Interpersonal Skills

For the first five years of her marriage, her mother-in-law dominated Eleanor's life. In 1908 Sara built adjoining houses on East 65th Street in New York City for herself and for Eleanor and Franklin. The houses had a common entrance, drawing and dining rooms that opened to each other, and a connecting door on the fourth floor. Sara had created nearly unrestricted access to her son's family. Not surprisingly, Eleanor took no interest in her new home. "I left everything to my mother-in-law and my husband. I was growing very dependent on my mother-in-law, requiring her help on almost every subject, and never thought of asking for anything which I felt would not meet with her approval."

But even with her circumscribed role, Eleanor held a deep attachment to her children, and coping with their crises, large and small, began to mold her as a person and a leader.

The greatest test of Eleanor's motherhood came in 1909. In March of that year her third child, Franklin Jr., was born. After spending the summer on Campobello Island, Eleanor moved the family to the estate at Hyde Park. While in New York City to see Franklin, she got an emergency message that all three children had the flu. Rushing back she found the baby particularly affected. He died, barely eight months old. "To this day, so many years later," Eleanor wrote in her autobiography, "I can stand by his tiny stone in the churchyard and see the little group of people gathered around his tiny coffin, and remember how cruel it seemed to leave him out there alone in the cold."

Did this image come back to Eleanor when, as first lady, she traveled to the desolate coalfields of West Virginia and saw children nearly starving to death? Did it help propel her to action and leadership for change that included creating new communities? Did her bitter self-recriminations over the baby's death contribute to a new level of commitment in her? Did dealing with her baby's death help her face future crises—both personal and political—with greater strength?

Of course, mothering meant smaller tests for Eleanor as well—the ordinary, day-to-day traumas that every parent experiences. Often, these difficulties revolved around clashes of personality between parent and child or between siblings. Although Sara forcefully overruled her daughter-in-law when it came to the children, she wasn't on hand for every blow-up. With five children relatively close in age, Eleanor had to do her share of negotiating, collaborating, mediating, and arbitrating between and among all sides.

The day-to-day replay in many situations of the two cookies, three children scenario is a mother-leader task familiar to mothers everywhere. Pamela Toutant, an essayist and management consultant, decided to stay home with her children when her daughter was born twelve years ago. Toutant still does some writing and occasional consulting, but her primary role is at home. With a boy and girl only two years apart, she does a fair share of mediating and arbitrating between them. She sees the skills she has built in this process as "transferable" to the workplace. "If motherhood doesn't give you the skills to deal with sometimes difficult people in challenging situations, what does?" Toutant asks.

Barbara Mossberg wrote about mothering as a collaborative process. "I like what Meryl Streep's character said in *The River Wild* when accused of favoring one child: 'I'm not on anybody's side. I'm a mother. I'm on everybody's side.' For me, a leader, someone with authority and responsibility for the whole, plays the unique role of being on everyone's side . . . . At the same time, the leader encourages investment and responsibility of everyone within the system, so that there is ultimate democratic participation . . . ."

In the Wellesley study, one woman told researchers, "If you can manage a group of small children, you can manage a group of bureaucrats . . . . It's partly team building. And a family is partly team building, too. Getting kids to work together and to feel the family feeling and not to be hitting each other and so forth." Another woman interviewed for the study, who was the middle child of six, saw herself as the leader of her younger siblings. "My mom called me 'little momma.' So I'd been born with sort of a leadership trait from day one . . . ."

Leadership is dependent on strong interpersonal skills, and the ability to build collaborative teams and environments is of the utmost importance. Mothering and care-taking roles are a proving ground for building these skills as surely as time spent in an office on similar tasks.

Values-Based Leadership Starts at Home

In *The Fifth Discipline*, Peter Senge argues that organizations should bring together the values that people hold within and outside the organization. "The conflict between work and home diminishes dramatically when the organization fosters values in alignment with people's own core, values that have equal meaning at work and at home."

Mother-leaders are keenly aware of their role as presenting and modeling the values that their children will incorporate for a lifetime. For Eleanor, in the context of her times, manners were an important consideration. She remembered expecting the impossible from one-year-old Anna. The baby had to learn to "sit on the sofa beside me while I poured tea with all kinds of good things on the tray. Her manners had to be so perfect that she would never even reach or ask for these forbidden goodies."

Of course, Eleanor had more realistic and serious values to impart as well, such as self-control, discipline, curiosity, concentration, being open to a broad view of people and ideas. To teach concentration Eleanor used a practice she learned from Mlle. Souvestre. She had the children lie flat on the floor after lunch, concentrate on relaxing their muscles, and listen while she read to them.

By 1927, Eleanor had formulated her list of "Ethics of Parents." She wrote:

1. Furnish an example in living.

2. Stop preaching ethics and morals.

3. Have a knowledge of life's problems and an imagination.

4. Stop shielding your children and clipping their wings.

5. Allow your children to develop along their own lines.

6. Don't prevent self-reliance and initiative.

7. Have vision yourself and bigness of soul.

Good advice for mothers, fathers, and leaders!

Today's mother-leaders look for the "teachable moment" to impart important lessons to their children. One such moment arose for me when my son was ten years old. His baseball league had a rule that restricted players to playing within that league and no other. Just before the season started, some parents on our team discovered that one of our players was registered under a false name and address to get around the one-league rule. Despite his status as one of the best players, we immediately told his parents that the application had to be corrected. They chose to withdraw him from our team. "But our league wouldn't have found out," my son told me later, "and we needed him on the team." This incident gave me a great opportunity to talk with my son about the importance of honesty over expediency, to emphasize focusing on values—doing the right thing, rather than focusing on success at any cost.

Mothers are typically the parent who spends the most time with children; thus they have the most opportunities for imparting values. These opportunities are subtle sometimes, and sometimes they stare you in the face. For example, when your child's friend abandons her for another, you have the chance to discuss the meaning of loyalty. When your son finds a credit card walking home from school and asks if he can use it, it's time to talk about honesty; and when you recognize the name on the card, it's time to talk about community. When your daughter asks why there's a lunch counter as an exhibit at the museum, it's an opening for a discussion of civil rights, freedom, and the meaning of equality.

Parents, especially mothers, have a unique opportunity to explore their values as they build the leadership and character of their children. In turn, children challenge parents to be more true to the values they promote. Those values are honed at home, travel with leaders into the workplace and become the basis of strong, effective leadership.

Mothers-Leaders Are Great Multitaskers

In a 1959 article for *Harper's Magazine*, Eleanor reflected on women's role as caretakers and what it brings to their lives. "The responsibilities of a family are, I think, excellent training in organizing one's life. Like most women, after my marriage I thought first of my husband and children . . . . Learning to fit my own activities into the family schedule was good preparation for the demands of work and public life in later years. Many women who are not married also carry family responsibilities, for an older relative or brothers or sister . . . . The self-discipline which these tasks develop is a great treasure for our later years."

Eleanor emerged as the dominant force in her household when Franklin won his bid to go to the New York state senate in 1910 and the family moved upstate to Albany, to a new home that would soon become a gathering place for political leaders from around the state. She found her chance to renegotiate her homebound role and her relationship with Sara. "For the first time I was going to live on my own . . . ." Eleanor remembered. "I think I knew that it was good for me. I wanted to be independent. I was beginning to realize that something within me craved to be an individual."

In Albany, Eleanor continued her role as family caretaker, but with a twist. "It was a wife's duty to be interested in whatever interested her husband," she said. Because political life was now Franklin's passion, Eleanor dutifully went to the senate and assembly chambers to listen to debates. She befriended the wives of other politicians. She saw up close, through her husband's fights with the Tammany Hall political machine, the inner workings of politics.

In addition to her roles as mother and homemaker, Eleanor stepped happily into this new life. Politics was a natural fit for the woman whose uncle had inspired a nation of young people to care about public service. She also became an interested and astute observer and an increasingly important sounding board for Franklin and his fast-moving career.

The Albany years began a period in Eleanor's life that mirrors that of many women at home today. Like many of today's mother-leaders, Eleanor combined volunteer work with household responsibilities. Despite her large household staff, Eleanor—now the mother of three—saw the children off to school, organized household tasks, met the children for lunch, and was home when they returned from school. She read to them regularly, took part in their outings, and supervised their bedtime rituals.

Each year, her large household shifted from New York City to Albany to summers in Campobello to the family estate in Hyde Park. According to Eleanor they were like "a small army on the march: a nurse for each of the three children, three to five other staff and a vast number of trunks, valises, hat boxes, and pets." But Eleanor had developed a reputation for efficiency. Sara wrote that Eleanor had to work "and think very hard before she got away and she seemed to remember everything, even tho' at one day's notice she moved a whole day earlier than planned." In addition to caring for her own family, Eleanor carried the added burden of being "mother" to her younger brother, Hall, who, like Eleanor, had been orphaned at a young age. Today we would say that Eleanor had a talent for multi-tasking.

Franklin's time in the state senate gave Eleanor her first chance to test her leadership talents. But the family's next move would present new and greater challenges.

In 1912, Woodrow Wilson became president and appointed Franklin assistant secretary of the navy. In addition to moving her three children to a new home in Washington, D.C., Eleanor had greater political responsibilities as the wife of a high-level presidential appointee. "I've paid sixty calls in Washington this week and been to a luncheon at the Marine barracks," Eleanor wrote her Aunt Maude. "I've received [visitors] one long afternoon next to Mrs. Daniels until my feet ached and my voice was gone . . . . We've been out to dinner every night."

Life in Albany had begun Eleanor's political education. Washington and the impending world war greatly expanded it. As she made her calls on the wives of senators, congressmen, Supreme Court justices, and naval personnel, Eleanor realized that her shyness "was wearing itself off rapidly."

Even though Eleanor had two more children—in 1914 and 1916—she no longer let pregnancy and childbirth eclipse her new roles. A month before her last son was born in March 1916, she gave a party for more than 200 people and was out and about nearly every night. One afternoon, when two senators' wives arrived for tea they were astonished to hear that the usually gracious Eleanor was unprepared. In short order they were led upstairs and received in the bedroom where Eleanor lay with her newborn baby.

In 1917, when the United States entered World War I, Eleanor threw herself into war work, and her "executive ability," as she called it, came to the fore. For her, being an executive meant organizing her five children for school and nanny care and entertaining friends and politicians in her home even as she threw herself into work for the troops. "My time was now completely filled with a variety of war activities, and I was learning to have a certain confidence in myself and in my ability to meet emergencies and deal with them," she wrote.

Eleanor worked in the Red Cross canteen in the railroad yards, doing everything from mopping floors to making coffee. She earned a scar but not a respite from her task when a run-in with the bread-cutting machine cut her finger to the bone. She organized a massive knitting project that provided bundled garments for soldiers overseas.

Eleanor's newly discovered gifts included a talent for advocacy, which she managed to find time for. When she visited the naval hospital she did more than bring flowers and cigarettes; she helped families obtain permissions for necessary treatment and expenses. After visiting St. Elizabeth's, the hospital for shell-shocked patients, she rushed to the secretary of the interior and pressed him to relieve the poor conditions at the facility. She begged the Red Cross to build a recreation room for the men and raised money to start occupational-therapy work in the new facility.

As World War I drew to a close, Eleanor continued to take on jobs outside her home while organizing her children's schooling and care and the demands of an upper-class household increasingly part of the intensely social political world of Washington. Eleanor acquired the ultimate multitasking reputation. Women who complained that they were unable to cope with the demands of their home and family were told, "Eleanor Roosevelt . . . has five children and moves them all six times a year—and does everything else besides."

Today's mothers have to juggle schedules, drive to multiple extracurricular activities, and keep up with everything from dental appointments to homework and school events—all without a staff! Planning and scheduling in a household is only a short step from planning and scheduling on work-based projects. Flexibility, thinking on your feet, and organizing are transferable skills—whether you're the only parent facing a field full of kids with no coach in sight, or a team leader whose key staff member doesn't show up for the client meeting. Mothers, the great multitaskers of our culture, learn the tools of leadership effectiveness in kitchens and on playgrounds and bring those tools into the working world.

ℰLEANOR'S WAY

- To talk about leadership, women need to use language authentic to their experiences.

- Women should not shy away from using mothering as a metaphor for leadership.

- What you learn as a mother is transferable to the workplace and will serve you well as a leader.

- Mothering is a testing ground for the leadership required to foster strong interpersonal relationships and collaboration.

- Organizational skills and leadership talents can be developed in the home as well as in the workplace.

- Mothering is an opportunity to teach and refine leadership values.

- Mother-leaders are great at multitasking, a key skill for any leader.

CHAPTER FOUR

Learning the Hard Way

"Readjustment is a kind of private revolution."

—ER

*O*n July 9, 1918, Franklin sailed to Europe in his role as assistant secretary of the Navy. Eleanor stayed alone in the sweltering Washington heat. She spent her days and nights working in the corrugated tin-roofed shack that served as the canteen in the Washington train yards where troop trains ferried the soldiers off to join the war effort. A fire burned in the old army kitchen as the volunteers fed the growing stream of soldiers headed overseas. "It was not an unusual thing for me to work from nine in the morning until one or two the next morning, and be back again by ten A.M. The nights were hot and it was possible to sleep only if you were exhausted," Eleanor wrote.

With Franklin out of the country, the summer of 1918 was probably the first in two years when Eleanor left Washington without having nagging doubts about Franklin. Two years before, in the summer of 1916, the first signs of a suspicious tension appeared between Eleanor and her husband. Franklin had been spending less time with the family at the summer retreat at Campobello; yet his demanding job seemed to justify his absence. Nevertheless, Eleanor began to have doubts about whether a different interest was keeping her husband in Washington—Lucy Mercer. Lucy was twenty-two years old and in need of a job when Eleanor hired her as a social secretary in 1914. With the relentless social responsibilities of an assistant secretary's wife, Eleanor needed help with schedules and correspondence. "I tried at first to do without a secretary, but found that it took me such endless hours to arrange my calling list, and answer and send invitations, that I finally engaged one for three mornings a week," Eleanor wrote in her autobiography. Lucy Mercer had all the organizational skills Eleanor needed. She also had the social grace to fill in the empty "female" chair at a dinner or lunch occasion. And gradually, Lucy developed a bantering, playful relationship with her employer's husband that evolved into something more.

In many ways Lucy possessed qualities that Eleanor lacked and Franklin craved. Where Eleanor tended to be judgmental, Lucy was an attentive listener, endlessly delighted to indulge the raconteur in Franklin. She carried conversations along, posing intelligent questions in her resonant contralto, her smile reminding people of the *Mona Lisa*. Eleanor's son Elliott remembered her as having "the same brand of charm as Father, and everybody who met her spoke of that."

In addition to her social charms, Lucy also was beautiful and cultured. Her mother, who had once been called "easily the most beautiful woman in Washington," had raised her daughter to glide through Washington's social swirl. Tall and straight-shouldered, with high-piled thick auburn hair and lively blue eyes, Lucy was a striking presence. Her paternal lineage included the founders of Maryland, and her education had been at elite schools, thus she easily fit into the upper crust of Washington society. However, when the family's finances and her parents' marriage foundered, Lucy's mother had made sure Lucy could earn a living as a social secretary.

By the summer of 1916 it was the Roosevelts' marriage that was in danger, and everyone in Washington seemed to know the truth except Eleanor. Franklin and Lucy took leisurely drives in the shadow of Virginia's Blue Ridge Mountains. While Eleanor minded the children during the summer at Campobello, Lucy often accompanied Franklin on sailing outings or out to dinner. Although other friends were included on these outings, seemingly as cover for the lovers, few people were fooled. Eleanor's cousin Alice, Uncle Theodore's first child, who carried an unexplained hateful bitterness toward Eleanor, was a notorious and inveterate gossipmonger who eagerly spread word of Franklin's attachment to Lucy. "I saw you twenty miles out in the country," she crowed to Franklin in a telephone call, completely unsympathetic to Eleanor. "You didn't see me. Your hands were on the wheel, but your eyes were on the perfectly lovely lady."

In the summer of 1917, Eleanor left for Campobello with the uneasy feeling that Franklin wanted her gone. He wrote her a typically cheery, reassuring letter, saying, "You were a goosy girl to think or even pretend to think that I don't want you here all summer." Then he continued his romance, cavalierly dining in public with Lucy, taking her to Cousin Alice's dinner parties and on long, romantic drives in the countryside.

The following year, Franklin took a trip overseas that kept him away from home for three months. In September, as Eleanor and Sara waited for his ship to reach home, they received an emergency telegram. Like many of the passengers on board, Franklin had become terribly ill in the deadly 1918 influenza epidemic. The women met the ship with a doctor and ambulance, and Franklin—suffering from the flu and double pneumonia—was whisked to his bed. His trunks and belongings from months overseas were left for Eleanor to organize.

When Eleanor turned to the task of unpacking Franklin's things and sorting his mail, a bundle of letters caught her eye. Lucy Mercer's familiar handwriting betrayed the correspondence as out of the ordinary. Why would Lucy have written so many letters to Franklin while he was away? Why did he neatly and carefully save this pile of mail? Eleanor began to read the letters, and years of suppressed suspicions were replaced with painful knowledge. Eleanor was brokenhearted. "The bottom dropped out of my own particular world and I faced myself, my surroundings, my world, honestly for the first time."

$\mathcal{R}$espond and Change

Eleanor was about to learn an important and very painful lesson: You do not and cannot control others. In fact, the harder you try to change other people's behavior, to make them act as you think they should, the less successful you will be. Even if they appear to change, they'll resent your controlling overtures and react in negative ways. Social psychologists call this response "compliance," a surface change in behavior as the result of reward or punishment that usually only lasts as long as the rewards or punishments matter to the recipient.

Eleanor coped as best she could, her inward struggle reflected in outward signs like her inability to hold down food and depressed moods. "Nothing ever happens to us except what happens in our minds," she wrote years later. "Unhappiness is an inward, not an outward, thing. It is as independent of circumstances as is happiness. Consider the truly happy people you know . . . . They have made themselves happy in spite of circumstances." So Eleanor struggled to hold onto happiness despite Franklin's behavior. Eleanor had discovered the basic principle of cognitive therapy. How one thinks about situations (or self) determines one's feelings.

Eleanor knew that she could not stop Franklin from seeing Lucy, despite desperately wishing for his loyalty. When Eleanor was away, she knew she could not make him answer her letters more fully, although she complained about it. She couldn't force him to come to Campobello, although she pleaded for him to. She couldn't stop Alice's humiliating chatter, although she likely knew it was going on. But she didn't collapse under the weight of her frustration and fear. She didn't stage furious scenes to try to force Franklin to act as she wished. Instead, she focused on her own growth. Perhaps the experience of seeing her mother try unsuccessfully to change her father's destructive life style led to Eleanor's inward focus. Perhaps her isolated and dream-filled childhood made her more able to look inward. Whatever the source of her decision, she turned away from recrimination and toward self-discovery. She found personal strength.

"Somewhere along the line of development we discover what we really are," she wrote to a friend years later, "and then we make our real decision for which we are responsible. Make that decision primarily for yourself because you can never really live anyone else's life, not even your child's." Eleanor went on to explain a central lesson of leadership: "The influence you exert is through your own life and what you become yourself."

What sets a leader apart is how he or she handles the lowest points, the darkest hours. "When life is too easy for us," Eleanor wrote, "we must beware or we may not be ready to meet the blows which sooner or later come to everyone, rich or poor." Like Eleanor, you should work toward self-mastery—the ability to take control on your own terms for the purpose of healing and helping yourself. That is how you will turn sorrow into strength.

As she stepped through the shadows of Franklin's deceit, Eleanor threw herself deeper into war work. She focused on building her independence and confidence. She learned, as you can, that the one person she could change was herself.

Reflect and Heal

Eleanor told Franklin to leave, to go to Lucy and marry her if he chose. If passion had been his only guide, Franklin probably would have left his wife, but his mother threatened to cut him off financially if he sought a divorce, and Louis Howe, his friend and political confidant, cautioned him that his political career would be ruined.

When Franklin expressed his desire to save the marriage, Eleanor laid down the terms: Franklin would never see Lucy again. Franklin accepted Eleanor's terms; however, this was a promise destined to fail. As he and Eleanor tried to repair their relationship, Eleanor wandered in the despair of her mind and heart. "There are times in everyone's life," she wrote, "when the wish to be done with the burdens and even the decisions of this life seems overwhelming." Caught in a canyon of misery, she spent long hours sitting among the graves of Rock Creek Cemetery on a northern hill beyond the U.S. Capitol.

Eleanor needed time to think, time to reconsider her future. Among the graves, a statue commonly known as Grief had been placed in a secluded grove of hollies. Eleanor sat on a stone bench facing the memorial—a woman cast in bronze draped and hooded, her face strong, lovely, and solemnly meditative. The historian Henry Adams built the memorial for his wife, Clover, in 1891 after she had killed herself by drinking arsenic. It was widely believed that her suicide was the result of learning of his love affair with another woman.

Perhaps Eleanor considered following Clover's course. After she discovered Franklin's duplicity, she found it hard to hold down food; she was uncharacteristically exhausted, beset by headaches, clearly depressed. But in the end she chose life, and something more: She chose "to take charge of her world. Nothing would remain the same," according to biographer Blanche Wiesen Cook.

Emotional recovery, especially of Eleanor's self-esteem, came painfully and slowly. Cousin Alice delighted in retelling a particularly pitiful story that occurred in the spring of 1919. Eleanor and Franklin were out at a party with friends at the elite Chevy Chase Club. These were the social occasions Eleanor liked least. She enjoyed serious discussions, but grew bored and irritable engaging in the banter and chitchat of a lively party. "I was always more comfortable with older people," Eleanor remembered, "and when I found myself with groups of gay, young people I still felt inadequate to meet them on their own gay, light terms."

The presence of Lucy Mercer made this party particularly difficult for Eleanor. As the story goes, Franklin stayed close to Lucy's side, and Eleanor peevishly decided to leave at ten. Franklin stayed behind, not returning home until three in the morning still merrily chatting with his friends. When he reached the house Eleanor rose from the doorstep, "looking like a string bean that had been raised in a cellar," according to Cousin Alice. She had forgotten her key and didn't want to disturb the servants. Evidently she couldn't bear the thought of returning to the party, but she told the group, "I knew you were all having such a glorious time, and I didn't want to spoil the fun." Instead she sat alone through the deep hours of the night waiting for Franklin's return.

Shortly after her devastating discovery about Franklin and Lucy, Eleanor clipped a poem from the newspaper. The clipping was found by her bedside when she died, the notation "1918" scrawled across the top. The poem, written by Virginia Moore, speaks of the devastation of deceit, but also of the personal redemption that can follow. The last stanza reads,

> *The soul that had believed,*
> *And was deceived*
> *Ends by believing more*
> *Than ever before.*

When faced with crises, it is important to take time to reflect as Eleanor did. Like Eleanor, you need to find your own place for quiet, uninterrupted thought. Using the wisdom of others' words, as Eleanor did with Moore's poem, can also be a strong salve. Leadership starts with self-leadership, with truly understanding yourself in every circumstance and finding your sources of strength. According to psychologist and author Howard Gardner, "Periods of isolation—some daily, some extending for months or even years—are as crucial in the lives of leaders as are immersions in a crowd."

Courage to Change

Over the next two years, Eleanor decisively broke free of any remaining vestiges of her mother-in-law's control over her life. She started by firing all of her servants in Washington, perhaps thinking they had conspired in covering up Franklin's affair. On January 1, 1919, Eleanor pushed her independence further, insisting on sailing overseas with Franklin for a postwar tour. Once there, she demanded to be part of every excursion despite the horrific devastation she saw.

In a gloomy church and monastery in Brest, France, that served as a hospital, Eleanor went to the garden in back where a tent for meningitis patients had been erected. "I was not allowed to go beyond the door of this tent," Eleanor wrote, "but it made me feel very unhappy to think how lonely those youngsters must be so far away from home and so seriously ill!" She visited battlefields at the front, trying to imagine the feelings of the soldiers "on the cold, gray, foggy morning that they, with full packs on their backs and rifles in their hands, plunged down one side of the canal and climbed up the other." The trip served as both education and emancipation for Eleanor's pent-up desire to learn and serve. She returned home with new determination to master "the domain of public service."

The death of Grandmother Hall in the spring of 1920 showed how much Eleanor had begun to reevaluate her life. "I wondered," Eleanor wrote of her grandmother, "if her life had been a little less centered in her family group, if that family group might not have been a great deal better off. If she had had some kind of life of her own, what would have been the result?"

Like Eleanor, Marni Court, a twenty-six-year-old editor at a general interest magazine, found the opportunity to grow and change after a major disappointment. It all started when Court told her boss that she was pregnant. Only two months along, Court wanted to give him time to find a temporary replacement. She planned on taking three months of unpaid leave. Her boss had other ideas.

"I can't keep your job open," he told her. "You'll change your mind and end up staying home." He went on to advise her to talk to her husband about her plans and to caution her against leaving her baby with a caretaker. Court reeled with disbelief and fear. She couldn't afford to lose her job. "Here I was, sick as a dog from throwing up four to five times a day, weak and dehydrated, trying my best because I'd been hoping for a promotion all this time, and I realized I had only a month or two, tops, to find a new job, because soon I would start showing." With a lawyer for a husband, she knew she might have a legal case, "but I needed a job, not a lawsuit," she said.

Court bought a new suit, applied for eight or nine jobs a week, and got the perfect new position in just three weeks. Her new employers appreciated her skill and were excited when they found out about the baby. Having dealt with the situation and succeeded showed Court that she had what it takes to "deal with a lot," she says now. "I didn't ever truly feel grown-up until this happened."

For Eleanor, turning disaster into courage meant facing her fear of an uncertain future with Franklin. "Courage is more exhilarating than fear," Eleanor advised later, "and in the long run it is easier. We do not have to become heroes overnight. Just a step at a time, meeting each thing that comes up, seeing it is not as dreadful as it appeared, discovering we have the strength to stare it down."

Accept Change and Take Action

In answer to the question "How do you recover from disaster?" Eleanor wrote: "You do it by meeting it and going on. From each you learn something, from each you acquire additional strength and confidence in yourself to meet the next one when it comes."

You will get stronger as you successfully negotiate the hard points of life, but only if you take action. Don't let yourself get "stuck" in the bad times. No matter how bad the situation, you can turn it around step by step if you are determined to follow your leadership passion. Tracey Manning, professor of psychology with over twenty-five years experience as a human relations consultant, explains the difference between life transition and life crisis. "A life transition is when you move from one way of thinking about yourself and interacting with others to another way of thinking about yourself and interacting with others. A life crisis is when you let rigidity or fear keep you from moving at all!"

Sally Velick had to meet a succession of tragedies on the way to fulfilling her leadership dreams. Velick had had an interest in politics since high school. She always felt the desire to give back to her community. She served on various planning and charter commissions, on the board of the Minnesota office of volunteer services, and on a state legislator's staff for many years. As her civic involvement increased so did her interest in holding office. She took the plunge in 1988, running against a five-term incumbent for state legislator.

Velick ran a competitive race, but as she was closing in on her opponent she got unbelievable news—her husband, Gary, a doctor, had a benign brain tumor. Velick's campaigning came to an abrupt halt as her husband began a series of surgeries and treatments for what turned out to be a recurring problem. Despite pulling out early, Velick got 46 percent of the vote and dreamed of a rematch. But her family nightmare continued. Gary had successive surgeries over the next nine years. Then another blow—Velick's son Aaron had sudden, unexplained kidney failure in 1996. As his kidney slowly deteriorated, Velick decided to become his donor, and a transplant took place. Compounding the traumas, Aaron developed lymphoma as a result of the anti-rejection drugs. Meanwhile, Gary's tumor returned. By 1999, Velick's husband was getting radiation treatments and her son was getting chemotherapy. If that wasn't bad enough, news came that her sister had breast cancer. Velick's life revolved around hospitals, doctors, and dreams of health. "My priority had to be my family," Velick said.

By 2001, with her son recovered, married, and the father of his first child, and her husband's tumors under control, Velick looked to politics again. "I really felt the need to keep my mind going. Illness makes you feel out of control, but these trials do make you stronger. You realize you can't just curl up and go away."

When Velick's retiring city councilman called and asked her to run, she said yes. She threw herself into the campaign, using all her skills from years of working in politics. "We had fun." Velick said. "People knew me from twenty-four years of being involved in the community. When I called for people to canvas door-to-door, sixty volunteers showed up!" In 2002, Velick took her seat on the St. Louis Park, Minnesota, city council just outside Minneapolis. She won with a whopping 78 percent of the vote.

As Velick discussed, your leadership ability will depend on staring down your fears and choosing to move forward with your life despite the obstacles. Eleanor advised, "We all create the person we become by our choices as we go through life." Leaders choose action over inaction; they choose to heal, recover, and move forward with life.

Understand that your choices will be challenged, as are every leader's, by time, place, and circumstance. Your company may fold. A capricious boss may try to make your life miserable. Personal tragedy may overwhelm you. Yet leadership grows not from having dreams come true, but from going through and overcoming setbacks. In the words of author Margaret Wheatley, you must be willing to work "with the forces of change." "Hurricanes, organizational crises, sudden accidents—these are terrible forces," Wheatley writes. But they can be the catalyst for change that becomes meaningful to us, that sparks new connections and relationships.

"People can surmount what seems to be total defeat, difficulties too great to be borne," Eleanor wrote, "but it requires a capacity to readjust endlessly to the changing conditions of life."

$\mathcal{E}$LEANOR'S WAY

- You cannot avoid your share of personal challenges, difficulties, and disasters. It is how you handle them that will determine how your leadership develops.

- Recognize and cultivate your capacity for resilience.

- Understand that you cannot change or control others; you can only change and control yourself.

- Strive for self-mastery—the ability to help and heal yourself by your own actions. Learn something new. Divert and redirect your energy in ways that build your self-esteem and abilities.

- Take time to reflect on your problems. Find a place that enhances your ability to concentrate and fully experience your feelings. Consider starting a journal. Recognize the importance of symbolism and history, and gather strength from the knowledge that human experience, like leadership, is universal.

- Search for optimism and affirmation in even the darkest experiences.

- Use the strength that develops from your sorrow to act. Be a leader in command of yourself, sustained and driven by the power of your experience.

CHAPTER FIVE

Find Your Leadership Passion

*"Work is easier to carry
if your heart is involved."*
—*ER*

*E*leanor swayed to the train's body-rattling rhythm as the countryside between New York and Colorado flashed by. She had joined FDR on his first campaign swing since he accepted the nomination as the Democratic vice-presidential candidate in 1920. So what if the Democrats had an uphill fight against Harding and Coolidge? Franklin had seized the chance to get his name known nationwide by running on the ticket with the obscure James M. Cox. Franklin looked forward to a vigorous battle, and he wanted Eleanor with him. After all, women had just won the right to vote and a candidate's wife could be a valuable asset in the election.

Eleanor agreed to help, but she grimaced at the sight of the smoke-filled rail cars where Franklin and his political cohorts drank, played cards, and plotted until late into the night. She had nothing to do, no one to talk to. She knitted, read, wrote letters, and fretted over Franklin's lack of sleep. Her only respites were the whistle-stops. Franklin warmed to his speech making, often becoming carried away by his own words. Eleanor listened with practiced attentiveness, but gave his coattail a hard tug when he needed to cut it short.

As the trip wore on over four long weeks, Franklin's closest political confidant, Louis Howe, noticed Eleanor's discomfort. He also sensed an opportunity. Bringing papers to her berth, he began to seek her advice on speeches and policy. He ignited her untapped interest and sought her friendship. Howe rightly recognized that Eleanor craved a political role and he had an instinct about her skills that would prove true. Thanks to Howe, Eleanor later said, she had been lucky to receive "an intensive education on this trip."

As expected, the Democrats collapsed in defeat in 1920. The Roosevelts moved back to New York, with Eleanor determined to avoid the meaningless social whirl of her mother-in-law's world. She found salvation just days after arriving home. Wealthy Republican and feminist activist Narcissa Cox Vanderlip appeared at Eleanor's door with an offer. The New York League of Women Voters needed her on its board of directors. Within weeks of accepting the position, Eleanor began running the national legislation committee, a job she took despite misgivings about her qualifications.

Eleanor suddenly found herself at the heart of a vibrant, committed community of women. They were smart, driven, bursting with possibilities after long years of fighting to get the vote. Many of them had come out of the social activist training ground of Jane Addams's Settlement House movement. They had worked at places like the Rivington Street Settlement, where Eleanor had volunteered after returning from Allenswood.

Many of the women reformers Eleanor met in the 1920s were extremely wealthy, and some were professionals, but they had walked picket lines, had marched in suffrage parades, and had gotten arrested alongside immigrant women fighting to organize unions. These networks of socially connected reformers were called the "New Women." Eleanor admired them; their energy and creativity impressed her and she quickly joined their ranks. "Their standards of work and their interests played a great part in what might be called 'the intensive education of Eleanor Roosevelt' during the next few years," she wrote in her autobiography.

The 1920s were the time when Eleanor found her leadership passion, her sense of mission. Her son wrote that his mother had become "filled with a passion for politics through which she saw the chance to right wrongs, to be of use."

All of Eleanor's experiences, all of her traumas and triumphs, successes and setbacks had led her to a driving desire to improve the lives of those less fortunate than she. "I think in some of us there is an urge to do certain things, and if we did not do them, we would feel that we were not fulfilling the job which we had been given opportunities and talents to do," Eleanor wrote.

Eleanor's words presage those of the psychologist Abraham Maslow who wrote about a need he called "self-actualization." "Even if...needs are satisfied," wrote Maslow, "we may still often (if not always) expect that a new discontent and restlessness will soon develop, unless the individual is doing what *he* or *she*, individually, is fitted for. Musicians must make music, artists must paint, poets must write if they are to be ultimately at peace with themselves. What humans *can* be, they *must* be. They must be true to their own nature."

Finding your leadership passion or mission means being true to your nature. It means finding your "certain thing" as Eleanor did.

You can be a leader in many venues and in many ways, but you will find your greatest opportunities for leadership when you have found the job, issue, situation, or cause that touches you deeply. When you do (and if you try hard enough, you *will*), your power to lead will flourish. You will get a greater understanding of yourself, other people, and the world. Finding your leadership passion may happen early in life or late, and what you are passionate about may change over time. The important thing is to discover and live your leadership passion as soon as you can, and as much as you can.

What Do You Value Most?

The first step in finding your leadership passion is thinking about what you value most. Your values have taken time to develop. They're based on your family background, religion, relationships, and experiences and they are a part of you. But unless your values have been tested they may not be apparent to you.

Eleanor felt, during Franklin's first campaign in 1910, that she "had no sense of values whatsoever." She had spent too many years judging what she wanted by what others— such as her grandmother, Franklin's mother, Franklin—told her to want or wanted for her. It took until the 1920s, when she was entering her forties, for Eleanor to feel that she was "drifting far afield from the old influences . . . thinking things out for myself and becoming an individual."

Certainly, there had been bumps along Eleanor's road to understanding herself. When she brought her new friends, such as Nancy Cook and Marion Dickerman (involved in a lesbian partnership), home to Hyde Park, her mother-in-law's disapproval filled the air. Rose Schneiderman, another new friend, also visited. A Jewish immigrant, Schneiderman organized women into unions and spoke militantly about class differences, leaving Sara aghast. Eleanor's refusal to abandon her new friends in the face of Sara's disapproval made clear her choice of reform work over the concerns of "society" and family. In choosing, she evaluated what was most important to her.

Eleanor also began to test her values. At a New York League of Women Voters convention in 1921, she decided to strike back at Vice President Calvin Coolidge's diatribe against women's colleges. Caught up in the anti-Communist red scare, Coolidge had labeled the colleges as hotbeds of radicalism and called the women Bolsheviks. Eleanor put in a resolution to condemn his outburst, but she didn't consider how the press would react. Given her status as the wife of the failed vice-presidential candidate who ran against Coolidge the previous year, the press portrayed her resolution as sour grapes. Although she felt "foolish," the incident toughened her resolve. In the future, Eleanor would repeatedly choose to follow her ideals despite the repercussions she faced.

Eleanor accepted the rough spots as part of her development. If she hadn't acted on her beliefs, if she hadn't tested the limits of her values, she explained, "perhaps I might have been saved some difficult experiences, but I have never regretted even my mistakes."

Eleanor's values eclipsed regret. Guided by a passion for justice, fairness, and equity, Eleanor began to lead her life in pursuit of fundamental principles. She urged others to do the same.

"To be mature you have to realize what you value most," she wrote in her 1960 book, *You Learn by Living*. "It is extraordinary to discover that comparatively few people reach this level of maturity. They seem never to have paused to consider what has value *for them*. They spend great effort and sometimes make great sacrifices for values that, fundamentally, meet no real needs of their own. Perhaps they have imbibed the values of their particular profession or job, of their community or their neighbors, of their parents or family. Not to arrive at a clear understanding of one's own values is a tragic waste. You have missed the whole point of what life is for."

There is no varnish on Eleanor's words. A clear understanding of your values is a prerequisite to achieving your dreams, to exercising powerful leadership. Values are the underpinning of your leadership passion. Can you lead without knowing what you stand for? Yes, but you won't make lasting and far-reaching change. Values underlie the motivation of all great leadership. As John W. Gardner writes, "The world is moved by highly motivated people—people who believe very strongly or who want something very much . . . . No human venture succeeds without strongly motivated men and women."

How do you clarify your values? Part of the answer lies in personal reflection and analysis, as discussed in the first chapter of this book. You must consider how early influences and experiences shaped who you are today. But understanding your values goes beyond deconstructing your past. You need to pay attention to what you do and how you feel each day. What captures your thoughts and imagination? Whom do you admire and why? Whom do you choose to spend time with? For instance, if you value creativity, creative people and events probably fascinate you. What do you read? What values do you want your children to have? What makes you happy and fulfilled? What leaves you sad and angry? Being moved on an emotional level is often connected with personal values being either honored or ignored. Think about how you live your life now to find clues to your deeply held values.

You also must ask yourself fundamental questions. What do you stand for as a person? Where is your moral center of gravity? What principles guide you? What values motivate you, give you energy, stimulate your creativity, ignite your emotions, trigger your empathy? U.S. Senator and presidential candidate Adlai Stevenson said of Eleanor, "She could not pass a starving person without feeling hunger." What moves you in the same way?

Perhaps you place a high value on independence, kindness, patience, or honesty. Maybe you're more moved by loyalty or concepts of fairness. You may have a strict sense of justice, or an abiding belief in inclusion and collaboration. Once you clarify your values, you can begin to search for your leadership passion.

Identifying Your Passion

In the summer of 1921, Franklin joined the family in Campobello in early August. They practically lived on the water—sailing, fishing, and swimming. But one evening just days after arriving, Franklin complained of feeling tired. He skipped supper and went straight to bed after a long day of sailing and a late afternoon swim in the land-locked Lake Glen Severn. "In retrospect," Eleanor wrote, "I realize that he had had no real rest since the war."

Franklin felt worse the next day. First his right leg gave way under him, then his left. Within three days his limbs were almost completely paralyzed from the hips down.

Excruciating pain racked his body. Eleanor became his round-the-clock nurse. "I kept on taking care of him and slept on the couch in his room at night," she wrote. "His temperature at times was very high. It required a certain amount of skilled nursing."

Arriving at Campobello, a famous specialist told the family the cruel diagnosis: infantile paralysis. Franklin had contracted polio on his beloved island. He would never again run in the sand alongside the Bay of Fundy, take long swims with his children, or even walk without assistance. He would spend most of his life in a wheelchair.

Slowly, painfully, and with heroic optimism, Franklin came to terms with his changed life. Eleanor was always at his side as the disease brought terrifying setbacks and shattered hopes. By the summer of 1922, a simple truth emerged—neither of them would let Franklin's disability stand in the way of their goals.

Franklin worked on his physical recovery and looked forward to a return to politics. Eleanor realized that her passion lay with her new friends fighting for social reform. She expanded her commitment to labor that had begun during her early years in New York City, joining the Women's Trade Union League to pursue her interest in improving working conditions for women. She became finance chair of the Democratic State Committee, giving advice to Women's Democratic clubs. Members of the Buffalo club asked Eleanor what she thought about trying to get a woman elected to public office. Let them run with "their ideals high," Eleanor advised, rather than just to win the seat. Try to find a seat where one woman has a chance to win this autumn, she advised.

Eleanor also actively backed Al Smith's campaign to win back the governorship in 1922. She rose rapidly to leadership positions, raising money, starting newsletters, debating, and going "Trooping for Democracy" with her women friends. Driving around the state, they pressed for public housing and playgrounds, better health care, shorter workdays, and protective labor laws.

In 1924 Eleanor went to the national Democratic convention as one of four at-large delegates from New York. She carried the planks that women wanted included in the party platform. "This was to be a new step in my education . . . . I was to see for the first time where the women stood when it came to a national convention. I shortly discovered that they were of very little importance. They stood outside the door of all-important meetings and waited. I did get my resolutions in, but how much consideration they got was veiled in mystery behind closed doors."

Returning to New York with a hard-won perspective on political power, Eleanor jumped into Al Smith's reelection campaign. Smith's rival was Eleanor's cousin, the Republican candidate Theodore Roosevelt, Jr., son of Eleanor's Uncle Ted, who had died five years earlier in 1919.

Eleanor welcomed the chance to score a victory against the scion of the Oyster Bay Roosevelt clan. Her Oyster Bay relatives had made derisive comments about Franklin during his vice-presidential run in 1920 and Eleanor intended to

ER with her father and brothers, 1892.

ER's coming-out portrait, 1902.

ER school portrait, 1898.

ER at Allenswood, 1900.

ER in her wedding dress, 1905

ER with her children in Hyde Park, 1911.

Marion Dickerman, Nancy Cook, and ER at Campobello, 1926.

Franklin and ER en route to D.C. on the back of a train, 1935.

ER with Lorena Hickok (*on right end*), 1933.

ER at a WPA camp, 1936.

ER at a WPA work site.

ER in Sydney, Australia, 1943.

ER with American women fliers in England, 1942.

ER in Bora Bora, 1943.

ER at Pearl Harbor, 1943.

ER in the Galápagos Islands, 1944.

turn the tables with a vengeance. An oil leasing transaction in 1921 by the secretary of the interior had resulted in criminal prosecutions and shattered the Warren G. Harding presidency. The oil reserves at Teapot Dome, Wyoming, had been secretly leased to private companies for the personal gain of Harding's appointees. "The recent Teapot Dome scandal—with which Theodore Roosevelt, Jr., had nothing to do—had created much excitement" Eleanor wrote, "so, capitalizing on this, we had a framework resembling a teapot, which spouted steam, built on top of an automobile and it led the procession of cars which toured the state, following the Republican candidate for governor wherever he went!" The gimmick of linking the Republican candidate with his party's scandal had worked. Despite a Republican landslide in the presidential election, Smith won reelection as governor of New York. Although Eleanor expressed some regrets about the incident in later years, it showed how far she had come on the road to being a tough political operator.

In 1926 Eleanor began teaching history and government at the Todhunter School for Girls that she had bought with her friends Marion Dickerman and Nancy Cook in New York City. She confronted the upper-class students with challenges such as "Give your reasons for or against allowing women to actively participate in the control of government, politics and office through the vote, as well as your reasons for or against women holding office in the government."

Eleanor had come out of the ordeal of Franklin's illness and become fully engaged in her public life. The leadership passion she rekindled in herself for social change would be her guiding force until she died.

If you are self-aware, in touch with your values, motivations, and goals, then your leadership passion or mission will become clear over time, as it did for Eleanor, and obstacles, even as terrible as Eleanor faced with Franklin's illness, will not stop your leadership. As you move into different jobs, different circles of friends, different communities, you'll be open to taking a leadership role when it feels right and important. Sometimes your reaction to an event will turn into a call to greater leadership. Sometimes small acts of leadership will grow unexpectedly and exponentially. Whatever the context, be watching for your leadership passion to come into focus.

Pam Miller, a forty-something single mom with a twelve-year-old daughter, took a small step on a vexing traffic problem in the fall of 2000. In a short time, and unexpectedly, she realized that she had found her mission—for that period in her life, at least.

Working part-time from home, Miller had watched in frustration as the traffic on her suburban street grew faster, louder, busier, and more dangerous. She tried stunts such as grabbing a hair dryer, putting on some khakis, and standing by the side of the street pointing her "radar gun," at cars to slow them down. But the last straw broke when her father, with Miller's daughter in the back seat, backed out of her driveway and was struck by a speeding driver right before

Miller's eyes. Both cars were totaled although miraculously no one was hurt.

"I got on the phone and called all over," Miller said. She begged and demanded that the local government do something, but she knew that everyone had to contribute to solving the traffic problem. She decided to plan a rally in her neighborhood and call it "Safe Neighborhood Day." "Government can't do it all," Miller said, "we're the rest of the equation . . . . We all have so much power to change things."

She only intended to rally on a nearby street corner, but word spread, and hundreds of people showed up for the rally. The press covered the event. Miller got calls for radio and television interviews. A second rally six months later drew an even bigger response. Strangers stopped her in the grocery to tell their stories of fighting the same problem. People started encouraging Miller to form a national organization.

While Miller isn't sure how big she wants the idea to grow, she knows with certainty that she's found her leadership passion. "I just hate the waste of life," she says. "Children and parents killed in accidents. I know how a life can change in a second, but this is such a controllable thing if we can get people involved." With tears in her voice, Miller concluded, "If I can save one life, it's a privilege."

Like Pam Miller, many leaders begin with dreams that arise from their environment. They proceed with incremental successes that feed bigger dreams. Their leadership is recognized and encouraged, and they encourage others to lead.

Live Your Passion

By the early 1920s, Eleanor hated the constraints of the family home in Hyde Park. Living under her mother-in-law's rules and critical eyes became increasingly intolerable. Eleanor longed for a place of her own. She wanted a retreat when her husband and children were away, a place to invite anyone she wanted, whenever she wanted. Franklin, Eleanor, and her friends Marion Dickerman and Nancy Cook, came up with the idea of giving her a piece of land near the main house. They agreed on a spot where he and Eleanor often had picnicked since his polio. He supervised the building of a cottage and a pool that he and the children enjoyed. But the property became Eleanor's treasured sanctuary. She named the woodsy spot after its brook—Val-Kill.

At Val-Kill, Eleanor started a furniture factory with Cook and Dickerman, an idea that Franklin had first proposed. Val-Kill Industries churned with activity as an experiment in "rural-urban balance"—a way to give workers in agricultural areas a livelihood during the winter months. While men and boys worked in the factory, Eleanor tried to get the local women interested in weaving and handiwork.

At Val-Kill, Eleanor's friends Marion Dickerman and Nancy Cook could live year round, and Eleanor could host her kind of parties—swimming, hiking, hot dogs on a grill. She and her friends had a place to plot and plan. They ran a newspaper called the *Women's Democratic News* funded by the state Democratic Party. By the time Franklin reemerged in politics, winning the governor's race in 1928, Eleanor had created for herself a life that made her fulfilled and happy.

Moving into the governor's mansion in Albany didn't distract Eleanor from her true passion. She told the *New York Times* that she would continue to teach at the Todhunter school. "I teach because I love it. I cannot give it up." She began publishing frankly feminist articles, writing in *Redbook* magazine that women had to "learn to play the [political] game as men do." She pressed the Democratic Women's Committee to work throughout the year, not just during election season. And she gave Franklin political advice, including successfully encouraging him to make Frances Perkins, a social reformer, the first woman in state history to become commissioner of labor.

Traveling around the state with Franklin, Eleanor also began her training as an investigator, going into institutions where Franklin's paralysis kept him out. She visited state institutions, went upstate to look at tree plantings, arrived unannounced at state hospitals for crippled children. "Walking was so difficult for him that he could not go inside an institution and get a real idea of how it was being run from the point of view of overcrowding, staff, food, and medical care. I was asked to take over this part of the inspection . . . . I learned to look into the cooking pots on the stove and to find out if the contents corresponded to the menu. I learned to notice whether the beds were too close together . . . . I learned to watch the patients' attitude toward the staff."

As Franklin's eyes and ears, Eleanor gained enormous power to move her social change agenda forward. As she reported back to Franklin she also wove in her recommendations.

Eleanor called other women to leadership. "If we are still a negligible factor, ignored and neglected, we must be prepared to admit in what we have ourselves failed." Her call is as relevant and clear today as it was in the late 1920s. Even as she sought out other women of passionate intensity like herself, she also sought to motivate more women to find their passion in life.

Your passion doesn't have to be connected to humanitarian goals, but it must be deeply personal and important to you. In *Soar with Your Strengths*, Don Clifton and Paula Nelson explain that finding a leadership mission or passion doesn't always require a big stage. "What of the mission of building quality into a Xerox machine or a Cadillac Seville? Or of helping people feel secure by having the right Northwestern Mutual life insurance, or the perfect stay at the Ritz Carlton or Marriott? Cannot the desire to provide quality to people in a product or service also be a meaningful mission? We say yes. Mission must first be personal. Your mission must mean the world to you. When put together with your strengths, it becomes your fuel for achievement."

After a lot of soul searching, former federal employee Juanita Weaver found her mission and the way to live it. Like Eleanor, Weaver's quest required determination and persistence, and is deeply connected to motivating others to lead.

Weaver spent two decades in the federal government, most of it in the Women's Division of the Small Business Administration. Although she was supporting the growth of women-owned firms, she began to feel that this wasn't her mission. An energetic woman with short grayish hair and thoughtful eyes, Weaver went to therapy, tried weekend workshops, and bought self-help books. She went to career counseling and interviewed other women she admired—nothing seemed to help her find what she was looking for. Then she went to a class on improvisation to shake herself up. "The first thing the teacher told us was that we were all valued, we were all artists and our time together would be a real relationship," Weaver said. With improv Weaver had to use her "total self" and "she discovered the "joy of creating." "I felt more alive than I'd ever felt," she said. "I felt I didn't need anything else."

Weaver started a quest to find a way to make a living bringing the insights of the creative process to others. She took an "early out" from the Small Business Administration, and launched into a fairly new field—creativity consulting. Her first client was the federal General Services Administration, and the training generated an article in *Fast Company* magazine. She has since trained private sector executives, entrepreneurs, and at-risk youth. "Creativity is an essential leadership skill," Weaver explains. It led her to her leadership passion, and she's using creativity to help others make the kind of discoveries that changed her life.

When you start living your leadership passion you will be swept forward, like Eleanor Roosevelt and Juanita Weaver, with the energy that comes from acting on authentic feelings and beliefs. You will carry a touchstone that gives you patience, persistence, conviction, and strength.

$\mathcal{B}$uild on Your Mission

Eleanor started her work with social change one child at a time at a settlement house in the Bowery in 1904. Over the next two decades she came to realize that social reform was her leadership mission. She built on her experiences and expanded the scope of that mission for the rest of her life. Why does a powerful mission often cause leaders to strive for new and greater goals? The "need for achievement," a need first measured by Harvard psychologist David McClelland, helps explain this kind of ambition and expanding mission. Eleanor exemplified the classic model of achievement motivation, which has three components. First, she constantly worked to overcome obstacles. Second, she always wanted to excel. Finally, she tried to reach the highest standards.

While some people seem to have a natural need for achievement, or achievement motivation, McClelland showed that it could also be taught. A strong sense of mission will help you develop your achievement motivation. Start by clearing out self-imposed barriers. Take the phrase "I can't" out of your vocabulary. Banish the word "should" from your speech and, instead, act on what truly motivates you. (Psychologist Albert Ellis called the practice of berating yourself with what you *should* have done "shoulding on yourself.") These negative habits get in the way of your strengths.

Build your achievement motivation by taking on challenging situations. Your challenge needs to be just beyond your grasp, not outrageously out of reach. Be optimistic about your success. Raise the bar for yourself, whether it's shooting for higher sales, conducting more in-depth research, or applying for the job that's a reach. Don't worry about what you "should" do; don't stop yourself with mind games about what you "can't" do—go get what you *want* believing that you *can*.

The period of the 1920s was Eleanor's time to shed the "shoulds" of her life and replace them with authentic desires. Her language, actions, relationships, and work became a total rejection of the "I can't" mentality. Her mission gave her strength to rebound from Franklin's illness, to literally build an independent life at her Val-Kill home, and to grow emotionally with new relationships and networks of like-minded women. She overcame her fear of public speaking, she wrote provocative published articles, and stood up to her critics in debates.

Don Clifton and Paula Nelson write, "Mission gives purpose to life. It adds meaning to what one does. In its purest form, it is so deeply felt that it explains why one does what one does. One's mission will touch the heart versus the head." Find your leadership passion. Act on the mission that will give you strength and purpose as a leader.

ELEANOR'S WAY

- Finding your leadership passion will depend on clarifying your values. Values motivate great leadership, underpin the actions that you take to build your leadership, and lead to lasting and transforming change.

- Leaders act within their environment. Every act of leadership based on your mission builds your capacity for making change on a larger and more transforming scale.

- Leaders can learn to develop their achievement motivation. This "need to achieve" means always challenging yourself, working to the highest standards and overcoming obstacles in your way.

- Take the phrase "I can't" out of your vocabulary. Nobody succeeds by expecting to fail.

- Take the word "should" out of your vocabulary. Act on your authentic wants and needs, not on those that are imposed by others.

- Find like-minded people who share your passion. Learn from each other, and teach each other.

- Finding your leadership passion will give you the perseverance, strength, and conviction to meet your goals.

- Never give up your quest to find your leadership passion.

CHAPTER SIX

Your Leadership
Your Way

"Women, whether subtly or vociferously, have always been a tremendous power in the destiny of the world . . . ."
—ER

"*I* never wanted to be a President's wife, and I don't want it now," Eleanor told her friend, reporter Lorena Hickok, in 1933. Eleanor spoke from her heart, but her public actions had been instrumental in Franklin's victory. She had worked on the front lines to ensure Franklin's win in the presidential race against Herbert Hoover. In the four years before, when her husband was governor, Eleanor became the most powerful political woman in New York state.

Throughout the 1920s, Eleanor and her women cohorts in the Democratic Party developed their political power in New York. The women took up the cause of progressive legislation. They were active in the Joint Legislative Conference, an organization that combined activists from the Women's Trade Union League, the League of Women Voters, the YWCA, and other organizations to work for progressive laws, especially for women and children.

Eleanor became chair of the conference in 1926. At meetings, rallies, and in the offices of legislators, she argued for an end to child labor, in favor of a minimum wage, and for a forty-eight-hour workweek. When Franklin became governor in 1928, she pressed him on these issues. The basement of her house became a classroom for women workers. She believed in the power of labor unions to change women's lives. With her friend Rose Schneiderman, the union organizer with fiery red hair and the passion to go with it, Eleanor marched in a union picket line.

Motoring around New York state with her friends in a green Buick, Eleanor gave speeches to bring women voters to the polls. She became the editor when the *Women's Democratic News* started publication. Striding into debates as the party's standard-bearer, Eleanor enjoyed vigorous verbal battles. She went on radio, began lecturing, and received requests to write articles. Her first piece for *Redbook* magazine was called "Women Must Learn to Play the Game as Men Do," and in it she told the women of America how to win political power. "Our means is to elect, accept and back women political bosses. To organize as women, but within the parties, in districts, counties and States just as men organize, and to pick efficient leaders . . . . Women are today ignored largely because they have no banded unity . . . ." Eleanor recognized the obstacles to women's progress, but she hoped to motivate women to overcome roadblocks and become leaders.

The article came out in April 1928. In November, Franklin was elected governor, and Democratic women got credit for putting him over the top. By his reelection in 1930, housewives flocked to the polls to vote for him. As Franklin eyed the presidential race, he wondered whether the 20 percent margin credited to women's votes in his New York race could materialize on a national scale. Determining that it could, in 1931 he looked to Eleanor to organize the women for his campaign. Jim Farley, New York State Democratic party chairman, was delighted. He called Eleanor "a strong and influential public figure in her own right." As historian Blanche Wiesen Cook wrote, "She had a following, and people relied on her views and depended on her leadership."

Eleanor decided it would be better to have Molly Dewson, her friend and a Democratic powerhouse, serve as the front person for the women's effort. Eleanor had become savvy about avoiding pitfalls with the press, and recognized that it wouldn't look good to have the governor's wife appear to be running a major piece of his presidential campaign. So Dewson kept up a massive correspondence with women across the nation—signing letters that Eleanor drafted. Dewson traveled and sent reports back to Eleanor who planned strategy. Working as a team, the two women pushed the concerns of female voters to the forefront in the campaign.

Eleanor openly worked the press for her husband, assisting reporters and writers who wanted to profile the candidate. She gave speeches, winning over Franklin's critics and gaining a greater following for herself. In November 1931, the *New York Times* reported on a dinner speech by Eleanor titled "The Individual's Responsibility to the Community." "Mrs. Roosevelt made many friends for herself and Governor Roosevelt. It was remarked by many political-minded folk at the dinner that she was a splendid advance agent . . . for her husband." Eleanor drove herself relentlessly, giving as many as nine speeches in three days.

Eleanor sent women to run campaign activities in every state and county, especially rural areas. She labored over work plans sent to her for review. She and her team wrote and printed millions of "Rainbow Fliers" to appeal to women voters. This was such a successful tactic that the men quickly began using the fliers as well. Women "grass trampers" went door-to-door to get out the women's vote. No woman had ever held such power in a presidential campaign as Eleanor did in FDR's 1932 race—certainly not the candidate's wife.

Her work paid off. In the midst of the deepening nationwide Depression, with food lines growing and fifteen million people unemployed, Franklin Roosevelt won the trust of the voters. The Roosevelts were headed to the White House.

Now that the campaigning work was over, Eleanor found herself on the brink of a new role—first lady. But she wanted to continue her political work, to use the influence she had gained, to be a leader working toward her vision for change. The traditional role of first lady as White House hostess seemed an unlikely venue for Eleanor's leadership to flourish.

Eleanor faced a test familiar to women leaders. Each new context, each new challenge presents the same question: How can I act on my leadership vision in a way that feels authentic to my leadership instincts? You'll face this question whether you're taking a new job, going to run a new department, taking office as a newly elected public official, or starting a business. As is often the case for women who want to be leaders but have ideas and ways of leading that are different than those who went before them, Eleanor had to blaze a new trail.

Research has shown that women often have different ways of leading and make different impacts on organizations than men. Judy Rosener, in her landmark book, *America's Competitive Secret: Women Managers*, identifies five areas where women's presence in leadership has the greatest impact. According to Rosener, women affect male behavior by raising the "level of consciousness" about women's issues. Women change power relationships because they are generally more willing to "empower others." Women have an impact on agenda setting, whether it's moving public policy toward family issues or focusing corporate attention on women consumers. Women tend to pay more attention to "the way things get done." Their preference for collaboration and consensus affects the management process. Finally, Rosener shows that women have an impact on the quantity and quality of benefits by asking for child care, elder care, flexible hours, job sharing, and other "perks."

Rosener found these impacts to be true whether the context involved entrepreneurs, government officials, or corporate executives. Therefore, whatever job you're in, you will have your unique impact as a woman leader by leading *your* way.

Claim Your Right to Be a Leader

Arriving in Washington, Eleanor scheduled a meeting with Mrs. Hoover to look over the White House. The first lady-elect refused a car or military escort from her hotel. She walked over on her own. After she and Franklin moved in to the White House, Eleanor impatiently dismissed the fawning attention of the host of helpers around her. Why should someone else run the elevator? She could handle it perfectly well, despite the protests of Ike Hoover, the chief usher, who was quickly being forced to look at women, if not first ladies, in a new light. Eleanor arranged her Val-Kill furniture in the White House herself. After all, she needed to get settled quickly and on to more important things. At the first large Roosevelt family dinner in the White House, the first lady passed on the opportunity for a grand entrance and greeted guests personally at the door. With small but noticeable acts, Eleanor signaled her intention to be a different kind of White House wife.

Just after the election, Eleanor had started work on two books, one about her father, the other a book that became part political call-to-arms and part homemaking advice aimed at women. Once in the White House, she continued writing for newspapers and magazines. She gave interviews, went on radio shows, traveled and spoke in countless venues. Was Eleanor a publicity hound and self-promoter? Some members of the press certainly thought so, but the newspaperman Heywood Broun saw her differently. "We are going to have a woman in the White House who feels that, like Ibsen's Nora, she is before all else a human being and that she has a right to her own individual career regardless of the prominence of her husband."

He was right. Eleanor was ready, as she put it, "to do things on my own, to use my own mind and abilities for my own aims." She felt more than a *right*; she felt a responsibility to continue her leadership on the social issues she had championed before FDR won the presidency. Eleanor wanted to have an impact on the White House agenda, and she understood that her influence depended on rallying the public to her side.

In September of 1933, reporter Rita Halle from *Good Housekeeping* magazine attended a conference on providing winter help for the needy. Eleanor followed a number of other speakers. The audience looked on, hot and exhausted. Then, as Eleanor began speaking, Halle wrote, "the wearied audience uncurved its collective spine until, all over the large room, men and women were sitting forward on their chairs in intent response to the magnetism of her simple sincerity."

Eleanor explained to her listeners that she had been called overly sentimental for believing that poor people required more and found loss and deprivation as difficult as anyone in any social class would. She rejected the idea that she was too soft or naïve. She told of having seen a child die from sleeping "on a cold, wet bed. He had slept on that bed because there were no panes in the windows and the rain came in." With the father unemployed, the family got evicted from the dilapidated place, and the baby died. "Yet people say that the poor do not suffer," Eleanor continued. "People who say that just don't think and don't know . . . ." Everyone in the room, including the hard-boiled reporters, responded deeply to Eleanor's words. Halle saw Eleanor as a woman who "had the courage to be herself and to do the things which seem right to her."

Like Eleanor, you need to be yourself, using your leadership in ways that are authentic to you. Eleanor made a bold attempt to lead in her own way when she agreed to accompany the Quakers on a tour of the coal-mining areas around Morgantown, West Virginia, soon after returning to Washington. There she encountered a whole region as wretched as any place in America. "There were men in that area who had been on relief for from three to five years and who had almost forgotten what it was like to have a job at which they could work for more than one or two days a week," Eleanor wrote. "There were children who did not know what it was to sit down at a table and eat a proper meal."

In 1931, at President Herbert Hoover's request the Quakers had begun a child-feeding program in the Pennsylvania and West Virginia coal-mining regions. This evolved into a larger program for subsistence living and vocational reeducation. Eleanor liked the Quaker idea of starting homestead projects, which would create economic independence for poor communities. People were put to work building their own homes and growing food on their own land. The men were encouraged to learn new skills and the women to revive "household arts." Attempts were made to attract new industry in the area.

Eleanor turned one of the homestead projects into her laboratory; she saw it as a demonstration for the whole country. It was a bold experiment in alleviating the desperate conditions in rural areas of the nation. Two hundred families were resettled on a piece of land called Arthurdale. Eleanor threw herself into the job of choosing the homestead families, overseeing the school and health clinic, even shopping for appliances. The government advanced $1.5 million dollars for the project, which the transplanted miners were to pay back. But efforts to find an industry for Arthurdale failed. Costs of resettling families in new homes skyrocketed well beyond initial estimates. In the end, Eleanor admitted that "there is no question that much money was spent, perhaps some of it unwisely."

In spite of the failure of Arthurdale, Eleanor had forced attention on rural poverty, a problem that the nation had long ignored. She had created the homestead project around her vision of shared work, shared responsibility, and collaborative decision-making. "If you care enough about certain things," Eleanor wrote, "and work for them, I think you are bound to find them in the people you are with." She had created hope for the miners, but, perhaps more important, she had demonstrated to the country a compassionate and interactive model of government action.

Like many women leaders today, Eleanor focused on the relational aspect of the problem—hoping to change the way the miners and their families felt about themselves, and to work and hope for change. Women, according to author and leadership scholar Judy Rosener, "see a connection between a collaborative and participatory process and more innovative and profitable outcomes. Men tend to associate a top-down process with effective management."

Writing in the *Chronicle of Higher Education*, a college administrator at The School of the Art Institute of Chicago, Carol Becker, explained her intentional approach to leading in a different way when she first took the job as dean of faculty. No woman had been dean in the school's 125-year history. "What could I do that might be different from the efforts of male deans of the past? What might a woman's leadership bring to this position and this institution?" she asked herself.

Becker's first thoughts went to relationships. She wanted a "healthy environment," which meant a place where women felt they "had the right to develop and assert themselves." That meant she would have to be assertive, proving to the women who watched her closely that she could handle confrontation or back stabbing from the men or the other women. Second, she wanted to create a team. She had seen male leaders grab credit they weren't due, she had seen blame wrongly shifted. "I wanted to communicate through my behavior that everyone was needed, and that together we could probably make almost anything happen." Finally, Becker made sure to listen. "I tried to transform a hierarchical organization into one in which people at all levels and in all positions could feel heard and respected," she explained.

Like Dean Becker, you need to challenge outdated leadership assumptions, you need to follow your instincts for leadership rather than trying to emulate old ideas like the "command-and-control" hierarchical model of male leadership.

The business world has shifted toward viewing effective leadership in the twenty-first century as highly interpersonal, relational, collaborative—in other words, people-oriented. Interestingly, it was a woman, Mary Parker Follett, who, in 1924, came up with the ideas that are gaining currency today. In a Wellesley College Center for Research on Women study titled "Inside Women's Power," Follett is credited with putting forward "the virtues of collaboration, coordination, sharing power and information, all of which are part of the current people-oriented, participatory approach to leadership."

Dean Becker writes, "Women must assume positions of leadership and act with conscious awareness of the significance of their roles. When they do, their presence can provide new models of leadership for everyone with whom they come in contact."

Shake Things Up

When women lead in ways that feel comfortable to them they often end up shaking things up. It is always difficult for organizations to accept new processes, challenges to hierarchy, different uses of power. Yet according to James Kouzes and Barry Posner's cutting-edge book, *The Leadership Challenge*, shaking things up is exactly what workplace leaders do.

Kouzes and Posner discuss five fundamental practices of exemplary leadership. They discovered these practices by looking at what leaders did when they were at their personal best. "Challenging the process" is the action that stands out first on the list. Who are the leaders who challenge the process? They are "pioneers—people who are willing to step out into the unknown. They're willing to take risks, to innovate, and experiment in order to find new and better ways of doing things."

This is why you can't let yourself be put off by the stagnant air of the status quo. Just because the work has been done in a similar way for years, is it best to continue doing it that way? Are there innovations that would benefit your organization, that would fit better with the organization's mission and yours? Can you see potential where others come up blank? Do you have ideas for new forms of organization, for new approaches? Women often bring a new perspective to their workplace that can start the ball rolling in new, creative ways. Being a woman in your position does make a difference, if only because the novelty of the change shakes up the context for everyone. Use that difference to your advantage. Put your ideas out there. Take leadership.

Popular culture has given some stirring examples of women leaders who took leadership by challenging the process. In the 1970s there was the film *Norma Rae*, featuring a fictional textile worker who rallied her co-workers to organize a union against the odds. Recently, Erin Brockovich became famous when a movie titled after her became a box office hit.

The movie chronicles the real-life exploits of Brockovich, who started out as a law office file clerk. Acting with curiosity and persistence, she uncovered evidence that a local corporation had poisoned a community through negligent practices. She had to convince her boss that she had found a case worth pursuing. That meant talking her way into the homes of potential plaintiffs, getting their stories, and winning their trust. She demonstrated her commitment, spending hours gathering information and analyzing it, all the while raising her two kids as a single mother. Her genuine concern for the people who were suffering, her honesty, and her tireless example gave the class of plaintiffs the courage they needed to pursue the action. At a critical point in the case Brockovich kept the group from falling apart as their trust in the process wavered. She repeatedly demonstrated the kind of relational strength that women leaders often display.

Brockovich chose to shake up the lawyer who was her new boss, the community, and corporate America. What she did took courage and conviction, two hallmarks of leadership. It also took a determined effort to challenge the process.

Eleanor liked to shake things up. "She shattered the ceremonial mold in which the role of the first lady had traditionally been fashioned," writes historian Doris Kearns Goodwin, "and reshaped it around her own skills and commitments to social reform."

Women's equality held a special place among Eleanor's commitments. That's why the Gridiron dinner caught her attention. The annual ritual brought the president and his cabinet together with newspapermen—no women—for dinner and laughs. So Eleanor organized a new tradition: the Gridiron Widows party. Newspaperwomen, wives of cabinet members, and Frances Perkins, the sole woman cabinet member, gathered to enjoy satirical skits and masquerades. Their revels often lasted longer than those of their male counterparts.

Sometimes, rather than shaking things up at your current job, you can create or fill a new job in an organization. This allows you greater opportunity to explore possibilities instead of dealing with barriers. Starting your own business offers similar freedom—which women must find appealing, because they are starting businesses at a rate nine times that of male entrepreneurs. If you have the choice, pick the opportunity that gives you the greatest freedom to use your leadership and follow your passion.

I once worked at a satellite office of Cornell University in New York state setting up training for workers, particularly women. I was the first one to fill the job. We were trying something new to help women clerical workers in state government break through the "glass ceiling." There were no predetermined "we've always done it this way" procedures to follow. While it was a greater challenge to find my way without a map, I also had greater freedom. Because no one was certain what would work, I could experiment. Working with the participants and my colleagues, I had the feeling of discovering my job, rather than just filling it. I was also able to build new networks and fashion a position that closely fit my interest in women's leadership. In twenty-first-century terms, in the "learning organization" that management theorist Peter Senge envisions, a new position gives you more freedom to be designer, steward, and teacher if you choose.

Obviously, you can't always find a newly created position, but if you do, you have the chance to be judged solely on your effort rather than against the previous jobholder's achievements or methods. If you've developed your achievement motivation, setting high goals and standards, you are likely to look like a real star.

In the 1980s, I went to work for an international labor union in the legal department. I quickly saw that the union had no one working on getting members involved in political campaigns. The union's convention was coming up, and I asked to be put on the political committee as a staff aide. Once there I suggested a new resolution recommending that a department be created to work on political action with the membership. The head of the committee thought it was a

LEADERSHIP THE ELEANOR ROOSEVELT WAY

good idea and asked me to draft the language. The resolution passed easily, and once I came back to the office I asked to be transferred to run the new department. Because I had suggested the change in the first place, the union officer in charge readily agreed. I had shaken up the status quo by using established procedures and set up exactly the job I wanted in the process.

Be Bold and Principled

It didn't take long for Eleanor to act on her vision as a first lady determined to make change. The alley slums of the Capital city were a disgrace and had been for more than fifty years. Filthy, rat-infested, plagued by disease and crime, these hidden houses were home to twelve thousand black residents and a thousand whites. Eleanor toured the tiny courts that held wooden tenements packed fifteen people to a room. Washington should be a model for the nation, she declared, and immediately set to work on a bill to improve the miserable conditions.

Eleanor met with community leaders; she lobbied Franklin's uncle who headed the planning commission for the Capital. She kept in touch with the residents she had met. Every Christmas after her family lit the Community Christmas Tree, she would go to the alleys. There she would help light another tree. "We sang carols," Eleanor remembered. "As I looked at the poor people about me I could not help wondering what Christmas could mean to those children."

Although the residents of the alley slums had a powerful advocate in Eleanor, that didn't mean change would come overnight. The "alley dwelling bill" she promoted to build new homes crawled through Congress. Even after its triumphant passage in June 1934, conditions changed slowly. For years Eleanor remained on the Washington housing committee and continued to lobby for housing, adequate sanitation, and improvements to fight homelessness.

Like every successful leader, Eleanor had to be persistent and principled in pushing for her vision, and so will you. There's no substitute for principled leadership. You must turn your values into action and not give up. This not only demonstrates commitment, it shows integrity and honesty. That's what others will be watching for.

Tackling a problem that others have ignored or avoided as intractable, as Eleanor did with the alley slums, demonstrates conviction. If you show your ability to see a job through to the end, to push past naysayers and overcome setbacks, you will demonstrate commitment to your vision. Coworkers will respect and follow your lead because they recognize that you are acting on your principles. If you falter and abandon your goals, they will view you with skepticism for the gap between what you say you believe and what you do, and they will be reluctant to support you.

Eleanor put such a high value on honesty that she listed it first in explaining what she considered the most important requirements for happiness. She felt that one must have "a feeling that you have been honest with yourself and those around you; a feeling that you have done the best you could . . . that you have the ability to love others . . . the feeling that you are, in some way, useful." Honesty is also the value most admired by others in evaluating leaders. Through surveys and case studies, Kouzes and Posner discovered that most people admire and would follow leaders who are honest, forward-looking, inspiring, and competent, with honesty being the highest-rated quality.

Honesty is reflected in the principled actions we take. Eleanor didn't just talk about helping the poor, she acted on her belief. She didn't make symbolic or token gestures; she focused on real, lasting changes. She didn't abandon her mission even when interim goals had been reached; instead, she held to a comprehensive vision of change and stayed involved to see it through.

Stick to the Mission

Although Eleanor greatly expanded the role of first lady, she stayed within the mission that enveloped FDR's White House. Similarly, your leadership must follow not only your own vision but also that of the organization of which you're a part. If you don't agree with the fundamental philosophy of your organization, or if your vision involves work that simply isn't done by your employer, you should consider finding another organization.

In the aftermath of the dot.com employment crash of the early 2000s, many workers have reevaluated their goals. Was their personal vision only about making money through whatever venture would succeed? For many, it wasn't. According to newspaper accounts, they've responded to an appeal from the Peace Corps to join in a different, and non-lucrative vision—hands-on help for people in Third World countries. These new volunteers wouldn't have made very good leaders in the Peace Corps when their mission was to make money. Conversely, they won't be suited to corporate leadership as long as their mission is focused on direct help for the poor. Leadership success comes from joining your vision with that of your organization and colleagues, whether you're in a boardroom or a bamboo hut.

Fortunately for Eleanor, she and her husband shared a profound concern for the poor, the jobless, and those struggling with the greatest economic depression the country had ever experienced. However, within that common mission Eleanor "represented the radical end of New Deal thinking," according to historian Blanche Wiesen Cook. She "embraced the needs of unorganized workers, the marginalized, and dispossessed: landless and migrant farm workers in the Southwest; sharecroppers in the Southeast; urban "slum" dwellers; domestic workers; uprooted and unemployed industrial workers—women and men."

Eleanor recognized that Franklin had political considerations that constrained him. Like every politician, the president had his eye on reelection. Eleanor didn't worry about such things, thus she was able to be what she called his "hairshirt." She scratched his conscience and often fought for more change, more quickly than Franklin thought possible or advisable.

An example of such a clash of interests came in 1933 when FDR endorsed as fiscally prudent the idea of firing married women before men in the federal workforce. FDR went along with a practice that had become routine during the Depression—using marital status as a standard for dismissal despite financial need or any other considerations. Eleanor thought it outrageous that marital status should determine whether a woman could keep her job. During the first two years of FDR's administration, thousands of women, nearly all in dire financial straits, were fired from their jobs. Eleanor protested vigorously, writing a chapter in her book *It's Up to the Women* that lambasted this practice. "Women's lives must be adjusted and arranged for in just the same way that men's lives are," she wrote. "Women may have to sacrifice certain things at times—so do men."

Eleanor had little luck in moving Franklin on this issue, but she continued to press for change. She and Molly Dewson, who had come to Washington to head the newly created women's division of the Democratic Party, had put together a list of women they hoped would be appointed to federal jobs. The most well known was Frances Perkins.

Eleanor wanted Franklin to make history by appointing Perkins as the first woman cabinet member. Perkins, who had known the president since his days in the New York State senate, had watched young girls jump to their deaths in the Triangle Shirtwaist Factory fire in Greenwich Village in 1911. An unstoppable social reformer, Perkins investigated the fire and helped pass the laws that sprang from public horror over the tragedy. She was part of the "Lady's Brain Trust" that included Eleanor in the 1920s, and Franklin had appointed her the first woman head of the state labor commission when he was governor. Perkins believed that FDR's New Deal had its roots in government's response to the Triangle fire, and she fought zealously to carry forward the reform legacy of that disaster. Franklin trusted Perkins and agreed to appoint her labor secretary. Her appointment represented a moment when FDR and Eleanor shared a vision that changed history.

Eleanor's strategy of working for the goals she cherished within the framework of FDR's White House is a great example of shaping your job while sticking to your organization's mission. If you're able to do this, your ability to lead will grow dramatically. Although not every effort will succeed, overall you will see the rewards of your ideas and actions. Your organization will benefit from your willingness to see and reach beyond conventional wisdom.

The millions of women who run their own businesses are particularly attuned to the challenge of sticking to a mission. As leaders they must put forward the mission, model it, and motivate their workers to follow it.

Korry Hetherington created a mission for her party tablecloths business, which she started in 1978: Provide the best service and quality in the region. Running the business has taught her about the challenge of leading a workforce in line with the company mission.

Hetherington employs nearly thirty people and currently has $1.5 million annual sales. "Keeping employees on track is the biggest worry. I learned I had to set standards, set the example of dealing with emergencies or irate customers. I also had to model resilience in the face of personal problems," Hetherington explained. "I'm divorced with three kids, but I don't bring the problems of that situation to the job. I tell my employees with similar issues, 'You have to keep your job. When you punch the clock you have to put it aside.' I judge my success by my low rate of employee turnover."

When a fire nearly destroyed Hetherington's business in the summer of 2001, Hetherington knew her employees were looking to her daily. "After the fire the employees had tears in their eyes every day. So I had to be strong. I had to come up with a game plan and act like I knew what I was doing, even if I didn't. Anything that happens, they look to me."

Hetherington used empathy balanced with keen business sense to keep her employees on board. She focused on her mission of customer service and quality, and her employees followed her lead. Her business rebounded and continued to flourish. Hetherington, like Eleanor, demonstrates how leaders, working within the mission of their organizations, can turn circumstances their way.

Today, women are becoming more confident about leading in ways that feel most comfortable and authentic to them. Using the examples of some of the top businesswomen in the country today, Esther Wachs Book writes in *The Best Man for the Job Is a Woman* that "gender-based characteristics for which [these women] were once ridiculed—a penchant for collaboration and fostering relationships—have become clear advantages at the office . . . . Women are setting the pace for new leadership." In the White House, Eleanor set a new pace, challenging the expectations of the traditional role she had inherited. Like her, you will find that practicing your leadership *your* way is the best route to reaching your goals.

ELEANOR'S WAY

- Women often lead differently than men. Follow your authentic instincts for leadership.

- Your leadership will be most effective if you stick to the mission of your organization.

- Leading your way may mean shaking things up, but that's what leaders often have to do.

- You can shake things up within the system by taking or creating a new job, which offers fewer restrictions and greater opportunity to be creative.

- Like all good leaders, you must "challenge the process" by questioning the status quo, looking for ways to be innovative, and exercising creativity. In this way, you can help your organization move ahead and succeed.

- Be bold and principled in implementing your vision.

- Stick to your principles and inspire others by acting on them. Demonstrate that you can be trusted and you will get the trust of those around you.

CHAPTER SEVEN

Give Voice to Your Leadership

"If you have something to say
you can say it."
—ER

*A*s veteran White House usher Ike Hoover looked on in astonished disapproval Eleanor Roosevelt carried a large box of candied fruit into the Red Room, ready to join the thirty-five women journalists assembled at her request. It was Monday, March 6, 1933, less than a week after FDR's inauguration as president of the United States. Eleanor had decided to hold the first on-the-record press conference by the wife of a president. Only women reporters were allowed to attend.

Eleanor held the event in the room where she had hung the portrait of her paternal grandfather, Theodore Roosevelt, known as "Greatheart." When Greatheart's son, Uncle Teddy, was president, he met in that very room with his cabinet. In 1899, President William McKinley sat in the same room to sign the treaty with Spain that ended the Spanish-American War. Now the echoes of past power and influence resonated around the gathering of astute and delighted women who held notebooks and pencils at the ready.

The Great Depression's impact on advertising and sales had forced newspapers and wire services to cut jobs, and because "newspaper girls," as they were called, mostly wrote features or society news, they expected to be the first laid off. But Eleanor's women-only rule gave the women a new "beat," making their jobs more secure. It also gave Eleanor the chance to control her own press in front of a sympathetic audience. She believed that, in addition to social events, there were significant issues "that the women reporters might write up better than the men." While White House veterans winced at the sound of shattering precedents, the first lady happily worked with her select press corps.

Eleanor launched her press scheme with, in her words, "fear and trembling." She faced an untried arena that many of her husband's advisers had cautioned her to avoid. Press secretary Steve Early grumbled that Eleanor might embarrass the president or disclose confidential information. But Eleanor's friend, Lorena Hickok, an Associated Press (AP) reporter herself, had suggested the plan, and both FDR and his close adviser Louis Howe had heartily approved. Eleanor later wrote, with characteristic understatement, that "there were many things, even connected with my own activities, which might be useful and interesting if well written up." She understood that the press could magnify her power to organize and motivate others, and she believed that the press routinely overlooked news that would interest women. In the interest of taking leadership on the issues she cared about, she decided to ignore the naysayers and her own trepidation.

As Eleanor greeted the women journalists, she passed around the candy to fill in the awkward moments as they found seats. Most of the women were strangers to her and she hoped they didn't notice her uncertainty. There weren't enough chairs and some of the journalists clustered on the carpet, giving male reporters, miffed at their exclusion, the chance to chortle over "docile news hens" who sat at Eleanor's feet. The men scoffed at the idea that they would even want to come to Eleanor's press conferences. The manager of the Associated Press said the gatherings wouldn't last six months.

"I feel that your position . . . ," Eleanor told the press women, "is to try to tell the women throughout the country what you think they should know . . . . You are the interpreters to the women of the country as to what goes on politically in the legislative national life and also what the social and personal life is at the White House." Eleanor laid the ground rules with uncompromising sternness. She wouldn't entertain political questions, as she intended to stay out of Franklin's domain and let the president handle national and international news. What was left? The world of social issues that consumed the first lady's life for the next twelve years.

The first substantive issue arose a few weeks after the press conferences began. Prohibition outlawed the sale of liquor, but Congress was considering a bill to allow the sale of three percent beer. Would you serve the beer at the White

House? the president was asked. "Ask Eleanor," he replied. Ruby Black of United Press International (UPI) rushed to catch Eleanor, a known teetotaler, at the airport. "Will you allow beer to be served at the White House?" she asked the first lady. "Ask my husband," Eleanor responded cautiously. She burst into laughter when told that Franklin had passed the question to her. She promised a statement at her next press conference. By the following Monday, male reporters were wishing they were "news hens" as they cornered their female colleagues and begged to be filled in.

Eleanor had laid the groundwork to control her message via an audience that was, at the least, understanding and, at best, sympathetic. Even so, she took additional precautions against misrepresentations. Her secretary, Malvina (Tommy) Thompson, always took notes. Eleanor also depended on two reporters, whose shorthand was impeccable, to provide a record in case of a dispute. She showed caution in controlling her message not only before but after she communicated it as well.

Ground rules about leaving political issues to Franklin soon went by the wayside. The first lady talked to the women journalists about sweatshops, urging women to boycott companies that failed to provide decent working conditions. She called for an end to child labor and for higher pay for teachers. She discussed the innovations of the New Deal—subsistence homesteads, work camps for single women, the National Youth Administration projects, paintings by Works

Progress Administration (WPA) artists and guidebooks by WPA writers. She shocked her press corps repeatedly by railing against isolationism. "We ought to be able to realize what people are up against in Europe . . . . We are in an ideal position to lead, if we will lead, because we have suffered less. Only a few years are left to work in. Everywhere over there is the dread of this war that may come."

Eleanor also used her press conferences as teaching opportunities, one day discussing recipes that were "patriotic, wholesome, and frugal," such as Eleanor's "7-cent luncheon" at the White House—hot stuffed eggs with tomato sauce, mashed potatoes, prune pudding, bread, and coffee. Her intent: to attack malnutrition and food shortages at the same time. "At the President's press conference, all the world's a stage," Bess Furman, an AP reporter and friend of Eleanor's, said, "At Mrs. Roosevelt's, all the world's a school."

Eleanor viewed her weekly meeting with reporters as a "battle of wits," and she found it challenging. As the 1940 election approached, they tried to trick her into revealing if FDR would run for a third term. "Where would you hang all these prints in Hyde Park?" they coyly asked. Eleanor recognized a ruse and avoided stumbling most of the time. Some of the women were protective of her as well, occasionally cautioning that a particular answer might be better off the record. But Eleanor had more savvy than the reporters knew. "Sometimes I say things," she told her press conference, "which I thoroughly understand are likely to cause unfavorable comment in some quarters, and perhaps you newspaper women think I should keep them off the record. What you don't understand is that perhaps I am making these statements on purpose to arouse controversy and thereby get the topics talked about and so get people to thinking about them."

Despite her fear of embarrassing herself or her husband, despite having the eyes of the nation on her, Eleanor understood that her leadership depended on being her own best spokesperson. Like Eleanor's, your leadership will depend on your willingness and ability to communicate your vision to others.

Content Plus Confidence Equals Effective Communication

Communicating effectively does not come naturally to every leader. On surveys of people's greatest fears, public speaking consistently ranks at or near the top. Fears about communicating can emerge whether you're addressing hundreds of people, a small but important group meeting, or a one-on-one that means a lot to you. Fear of speaking in public may cause your breath to get short or your heart to pound or may make you sweat. All of these reactions can be controlled, and even turned to your advantage with practice. However, becoming a good public speaker isn't the only element in effective communications; it also requires savviness about choosing the time, place, and audience, and careful preparation to maximize the opportunity to motivate people.

Eleanor's strategic use of the press, her self-assurance about her public image, and her bold public presence on issues came from years of practice and her fair share of slips and falls. Over time she developed political antennae that led her to fashion and target her message for the greatest impact.

When Franklin got the nomination for vice president at the Democratic convention in San Francisco in 1920, not much was known about his wife. The Washington society reporter for the *New York Times* described her as "essentially a home woman. She seems to particularly dislike the official limelight." Eleanor refused to send a picture to Louis Howe to give to newspapers in Washington because she thought of herself as ugly. Correspondents went to interview Eleanor at the family's summer retreat on Campobello Island off the coast of Maine, but found her stilted and brief. The reporters left the remote retreat with little to take back to their editors.

During the 1920 campaign, when Eleanor accompanied Franklin on campaign tours, Louis Howe broke through her reluctance to deal with the press. He explained how the press operated and encouraged her to make friends with reporters. By the end of the trip, she was comfortable enough to joke with reporters at campaign stops.

Franklin and his party lost the 1920 election, but Eleanor's political apprenticeship had begun. She became active in the League of Women Voters and soon joined the board. Eleanor began to speak at League luncheons on issues such as giving equal representation to men and women at all levels. Although Eleanor was finally willing to speak before an audience, her speaking skills were poor. Her odd voice and cadence would cause unexpected high notes; she appeared painfully self-conscious and giggled nervously. "Stop that," Louis Howe would growl at Eleanor. He came to meetings and gave her curt advice, such as "Have something to say, say it, and then sit down." She learned to hold the podium to still her shaking hands, to smile and take a deep breath to quell her nervousness. She worked at being prepared so she could be confident. She learned to make eye contact with her audience. Voice trainers were hired to modulate her speech. Gradually the nervous laughter disappeared and Eleanor became a gifted and sought-after speaker.

Eleanor's example shows that it's possible to learn to be a better communicator. She learned to give lectures and speeches from a single page of notes. By 1935, she gave a message to students of public speaking that echoed her mentor Louis Howe, "Have something to say, say it and sit down." She also advised them to "write out the beginning and the end of a speech. Use notes and think out a speech, but never write it down." She only liked to speak when she could be inspiring and helpful, when she could fill her speeches with the moral purpose that guided her. Although she often challenged her listeners, her grace and modesty never failed her. "Be conciliatory, never antagonistic, toward your audience," she advised, "or it may disagree with you, no matter what you say."

Eleanor's strength as a speaker grew. She electrified audiences. She had to hire an agent to manage her speaking engagements. "She's got a message," said one woman who had waited over an hour to get into one of Eleanor's lectures, "and gosh! She's given it to 'em hot!"

As a leader, you can aspire to Eleanor's mastery of the public stage. Like her, you can practice, overcome your fears, and communicate with confidence. "You must speak in a convincing and unconditional manner," Gail Evans writes in *Play Like a Man/Win Like a Woman.* "If you have to, go home and talk to a blank wall," she advises. "Say, 'I've had enough .... I won't be cut off in the meetings anymore.' Speak loudly enough so that if there were someone in the room, no matter where he or she was, you could be heard." Evans, a former CNN executive, says women "speak from the place called nopermission," and recommends that women take a course in presentation skills.

Look for situations to make presentations, practice in front of friends or relatives and the mirror. Join an organization like the Toastmasters clubs where you can have opportunities to practice speaking on a regular basis in a supportive environment. Have a goal in mind based on an assessment of your speaking skills. Assess yourself honestly and look for honest feedback. Are you too slow to get to the point in a time-limited setting? If you're trying to influence someone one-on-one, are you good at asking for what you want or closing the deal? When addressing a large group, do you consider who your audience is and tailor your remarks effectively?

There are many great books and Web sites with advice on public speaking as a personal skill. Like Eleanor, with practice and attention to what you need to improve, you can build your ability to communicate effectively.

Learning to communicate effectively also means planning for what will be communicated, when it will be communicated, and to whom. Angela Airall, a consulting director with learning services at Johnson & Johnson approaches communications as a marketing venture. She says, "communications is about knowing your audience and helping to unleash them to step out of their comfort zone."

Under the direction of JoAnn Heffernan Heisen, the only woman on the J&J board and the company's CIO, Airall worked with teams from several of J&J's operating companies to write the business case for the women's leadership initiative. The initiative had to be sold within J&J to its operating boards representing companies like Neutrogena, Janssen, and other well-known brands. The business case had to communicate that the advancement of women inside the company would provide needed insight on women consumers, who are J&J's most important customers.

During the design and planning stages of the initiative, Airall helped her teams find what she called their "conversational courage." She helped the group devise a communication plan that wove a powerful story about career advancement while persuading their stakeholders to rethink assumptions. The team agreed the initiative required a communication plan centered on authentic conversation about substantive issues.

Key stakeholders were identified. The team spoke with different ethnic groups and non-U.S. based staff members to publicize the initiative and garner worldwide support. (J&J has 101,800 employees and 197 operating companies in 54 countries around the world.) Airall explained, "We designed a toolkit with scripts, meeting agendas, an introductory one-sheet, and other support materials. We created an 'initiative-in-a-box' that could be customized to the particular needs and culture of each operating company." As endorsements by senior executives grew, the initiative's programs were cascaded down through different organizations and departments. According to Airall, "As directors volunteered their support, a wave of courage and insight flowed throughout J&J's operating companies. Without a purposeful communication plan, the initiative would have evaporated into the corporate clouds."

Every project requires not only your personal skill as a communicator, but the kind of planning for effective communications that Airall was part of at Johnson & Johnson.

Cultivate Creative Communications Strategies

Without any formal authority, Eleanor's leadership depended on her ability to influence the public. How could she get her views more widely known? Radio shows were becoming popular, and after Franklin won the governorship of New York in 1928, Eleanor began a sponsored radio program presenting the woman's view on a range of topics. She also started lecturing around the state. Always a prolific writer, she began writing articles for magazines—"What I Want Most Out of Life" for *Success Magazine*, "Why Democrats Favor Smith" for the *North American Review*, "The Modern Wife's Difficult Job" for *The Literary Digest*. Eleanor's travels also got her publicity. She donned a miner's hat and rode a coal car into a mine. She sat with impoverished families in their kitchens sipping tea and listening to their problems. She knew the press would cover her travels, which meant that her choices of where to show up would carry communications value. For instance, in 1934 several women journalists accompanied her on a much-publicized trip to Puerto Rico and the U.S. Virgin Islands in March. Within weeks, Americans were reading about poverty in the territories. "ER's visit set in motion the beginnings of the New Deal for the islands," wrote Blanche Wiesen Cook.

By the end of the 1920s, Eleanor had developed political savvy and an arsenal of knowledge about public relations. Her exposure as a candidate's wife and as a political activist had helped her realize the powerful effect she had on strangers. Her empathy and sincerity, her ability to listen and respond simply and sensitively, and her openness and lack of arrogance all contributed to her ability to win over strangers—and be a leader on the political scene.

Speaking to your constituency using multiple venues, as Eleanor did, is part of being a creative communicator. Eleanor would clearly have a Web site if she were alive today. Another part of creative communications has to do with the content of your message.

In 1995, Martha Lee invited fifteen women to Aspen, Colorado, to discuss the need for an organization that would enhance the leadership capacity of Asian American and Pacific Islander women. Over the course of two days this group of nationally known Asian American and Pacific Islander women made a collective decision to move forward. "We came up with a plan," Lee explained, "to each ask fifteen people for one hundred dollars to see if there was interest." Soon after the meeting ended the money started pouring in. "The initial group of one hundred women has grown to over four hundred sisters," Lee says, "who contribute financially so AAPI women can learn ethical, caring, and compassionate ways of leading."

How did Lee do it? Lee says she tries to be conscious of her audience. "You talk to your grandmother differently than to your mother," she says. She often uses metaphor and imagery to invite people to join in her vision. "You have to paint a picture—that's how people decide to work with you. Make them feel they're inside the dream, they are part of the dream and the dream can become reality. Show them the trees, the fields, the story of the river." Lee's brochure for the organization's national summit leads off with a poem titled "Sisters, Let Us Gather at the River." For Lee's group the river is the metaphor for movement and for "a place of peace, a place of commerce, a place where you met each other, a place where you shared stories over washing laundry . . . a place of dreams."

Lee's approach in communicating about her organization is both creative and attuned to the cultural background of her audience. As she says, "You can't take a cookie cutter approach to communications." Like Lee, you can learn to communicate with facts as well as emotions and symbols.

Author and business leader Warren Bennis writes about the effectiveness of leaders who use verbal metaphors, as well as those who literally draw pictures. "The actions and symbols of leadership frame and mobilize meaning," Bennis writes. "Leaders articulate and define what has previously remained implicit and unsaid; then they invent images, metaphors, and models that provide a focus for new attention." There are no limits to the ways that you can creatively communicate to those you're trying to influence as a leader.

*D*on't Hide Your Light

When she became first lady, Eleanor used the national stage to showcase communications skills she had learned in New York State. She skillfully wove her use of media with the power of her personal relationships and appearances. Despite being the president's wife, she didn't let FDR eclipse her. She delighted in the fact that her historic first press conference had beat his first press conference by three days.

In July 1933 Eleanor took on a monthly column for the *Woman's Home Companion* and titled her first piece "I Want You to Write Me." She didn't have to ask twice. By January 1934, she had received three hundred thousand letters. According to historian Allida Black, this flood of correspondence exceeded the total received by Abraham Lincoln and Woodrow Wilson in their first years in office—combined! Housewives, the lovelorn, teachers, employers, children, the elderly wrote to the First Lady. Eleanor's massive correspondence, her articles, press conferences, and speeches had made her "a personality in her own right . . . [with] an independent course of instruction on her own account," notes historian Mary Beard.

In 1935 Eleanor extended her outreach. She agreed to do a syndicated column six days a week for United Features called "My Day." Her first "My Day" column in January 1936 was a chatty memoir of the Christmas holidays, describing the excitement of the children, Franklin's head cold, and the conversation that accompanied a large family lunch. In later columns she revealed her personality in snippets such as, "I sallied forth and in two brief hours ordered all my winter clothes." She discussed books and plays of the time.

Eleanor had become, in the words of a reporter at the time, "a cabinet minister without portfolio," thanks to her skill at communicating her message through the many avenues she developed. By the end of FDR's first one hundred days, the hope returning to a beleaguered country came not only from the president's decisive actions but also from the unexpected leadership of the first lady.

Years later, after FDR died in 1945, the new president, Harry Truman, and his wife Bess were on the funeral train to Washington. Eleanor offered the new first lady public relations advice. Hold a press conference this week, she urged. With her usual generosity, Eleanor offered to sit by Mrs. Truman's side and introduce her to the women reporters. "Do you think I ought to do that?" Bess Truman asked Labor Secretary Frances Perkins. "It terrifies me. I don't even think of public affairs." "No, Mrs. Truman," Perkins replied. "I don't think you ought to feel the slightest obligation to do it. Mrs. Roosevelt is an unusual person. She enjoys it. There certainly isn't anything the press has a right to ask you."

Mrs. Truman's question and Perkins's answer reflected an outmoded attitude. The press had gained tremendous power in the years of FDR's presidency. Eleanor had learned to think in terms of what she had a right to demand from the press rather than the other way around. Her attitude toward mass media, one that would be repeated and magnified by leaders throughout the rest of the century, gave her leadership power she could not have achieved any other way. She had never been elected to any position, but Eleanor had made herself into a public person of enormous influence through communicating her mission and message.

Eleanor succeeded because she didn't hide her light under a bushel. Follow her example by creating attention for your vision and not letting others steal or overshadow your initiative. If your leadership ideas are important to you, let your actions show it. Talk about your ideas, write about them, get them in the company newsletter—do all these things if possible—and do them more than once. Repetition works because what's important to you is not necessarily important to anyone else; therefore, other people need to be reminded about your priorities. Speak up at meetings, corner the right people and communicate your message. Be creative, have a clear message, use humor, and be persistent.

It's also important to choose your moments to shine light on your vision or ideas. Eleanor's "My Day" column carried many political messages. "It seems to me that the Prime Minister of England did a fine thing," she wrote in September 1938, "when he went to visit the German Chancellor in a last effort to prevent bloodshed." She also talked about less weighty subjects, such as an unconventional lunch she had with the royal family. "Oh dear, oh dear," Eleanor wrote in May 1939, "so many people are worried that 'the dignity of our country will be imperiled' by inviting royalty to a picnic, particularly a hot dog picnic." Eleanor believed that "too much crusading for a cause is almost as bad as too little," concerned that, "people get weary of too much preaching." Pick the time, place, and way to communicate as you push your ideas to the forefront.

Eleanor guarded the public attention she had earned—even against encroachment by Franklin. When she came down with a severe cold and fever in September 1936, Franklin was worried enough to stop campaigning and return to her bedside. He offered to give her a break and write her "My Day" column. Instead, Eleanor informed her readers of her husband's offer saying she "refused courteously and rapidly knowing that if it once became the President's column we would lose our readers . . . ."

Eleanor claimed independent leadership, shining her own light rather than staying in Franklin's shadow. She gave permission to every woman leader to build her own power and leadership.

Communicate from Your Heart

Columnists, even some who disliked Eleanor, admitted that her style and public presence helped the president. They were astonished that after her speeches she subjected herself to grueling questions and handled them so ably. Eleanor regularly took written questions passed up by the audience and read them aloud. At a lecture in Akron, Ohio, in 1938, she got an unexpectedly harsh inquiry. "Do you think your husband's illness has affected your husband's mentality?" Eleanor read with no apparent show of emotion. "I am glad that question was asked," she said, as the audience seemed to hold its breath. "The answer is yes. Anyone who has gone through great suffering is bound to have a greater sympathy and understanding of the problems of mankind." The audience rose in a standing ovation.

Eleanor's own sympathy and understanding overflowed, leading her to communicate in ways that were previously unimaginable for a first lady. In 1933, for example, a group of rag-tag World War I veterans marched into Washington for the second year in a row, demanding payment of their veterans' bonuses. The year before, President Hoover had ordered tanks and tear gas to blast them out of the squatters' shacks they had occupied. FDR opposed the bonuses too, instead encouraging the men to go to work for the Civilian Conservation Corps (CCC) for a dollar a day. Insulted by the offer, the men grew more incensed. They settled uneasily into an encampment at Fort Hunt, about twelve miles from Washington. Eleanor encouraged FDR to arrange a meager campsite and meals for the veterans. FDR had even driven out to the camp, waving from his car and ordering hot coffee for all, but the situation remained tense.

Louis Howe talked to the veterans' leaders daily, and he came up with an idea. He suggested to Eleanor that she accompany him on a visit to the "bonus army"—as the veterans had come to be known. But when they arrived at the campsite, Howe stayed in the car. The first lady waded into the ankle-deep mud, hesitant but prepared to face the men alone. She told them she had no answer for their demands but had come to see how they were getting on. They walked her around the barracks and hospital, ending up in the mess hall, where Eleanor gave an impromptu speech. She talked of her work in the canteens, of visiting the battlefields after the war. "I never want to see another war. I would like to see fair consideration for everyone, and I shall always be grateful to those who served their country." Then she led the men in singing some of their favorites songs, such as the sentimental tune "There's a Long, Long Trail." She departed to cheers. Until Eleanor visited, the men didn't believe "there was a dime's worth of difference between Hoover and Roosevelt," according to historian Blanche Wiesen Cook. Within a few days, they had dispersed, more than twenty-five hundred of them eventually taking jobs with the CCC. Word of her visit spread. "It is such fine things as that," former Secretary of the Navy Josephus Daniels wrote to Eleanor from Mexico, "which bring you the admiration of the American people."

All of the practice, thought, and planning that go into your communications as a leader will be worthless if you don't communicate from your heart. Your greatest communications asset is authenticity, because it will allow other people to feel the emotional energy you bring to your message and be moved to act in turn.

ELEANOR'S WAY

- Learn to be an effective personal communicator by getting honest feedback and honestly assessing your communications skills. Then use practice to improve.

- Search for new ways to reach your audience to communicate your leadership messages.

- Take your message to the audience you need to reach. The exact opportunity to communicate about yourself or your idea isn't likely to come to you.

- Show creativity in the content of your communications. Don't take a "cookie-cutter approach." Every situation presents new challenges for creative communication.

- Show your sincerity and passion as you communicate in both words and images. If you don't have the conviction to support your idea no one else will either.

- Don't hide your light behind anything or anyone.

CHAPTER EIGHT

Face Criticism with Courage

"Develop a skin as thick
as a rhinoceros hide!"
—ER

*E*arly in FDR's first term as president, Eleanor agreed to teach a civics course for the women members of the New York Junior League. At her first lecture she faced a crowded auditorium filled with several hundred debutantes and women from high society. Eleanor strode to the lectern. She likely had her thick, wavy hair pulled into a bun. She often wore a large corsage and a big bow on her neckline. A year away from her fiftieth birthday, Eleanor's figure had thickened but, with her long legs and neck, she still towered gracefully over most of her colleagues. She smiled often and broadly, but she had a serious message for her audience.

The League had a history of trying to bridge the gap of class by sending its members to help the needy. Eleanor's friend Mary Harriman Rumsey, the wealthy daughter of a railroad financier, had laid the foundation for the League when she gathered her friends together to teach immigrants in evening classes. By joining the League, members turned their attention from the comfort of wealth to the conflicts of social change. Eleanor hoped to encourage this audience to do the same.

If government didn't help people who were starving and cold and unemployed, Eleanor told the women, everyone would feel the consequences. She wanted her audience to understand that desperate people often take desperate measures. She had been to Appalachia and seen people living in flimsy shacks, subsisting on scraps, and having no prospects for work. She reminded these wealthy women of the thousands of young Americans with no work and no prospects for the future. She told them the story of a man who had gone to jail for stealing food for his family. When he was released for good behavior, the man told the warden he wouldn't hesitate to repeat his crime. "I wouldn't blame him," Eleanor concluded. "You would be a poor wishy-washy sort of person if you didn't take anything you could when your family was starving." Such stories had galvanized audiences in the past, but however moved the Junior Leaguers were to take up Eleanor's challenge, the press and public had a different reaction.

Editorial pages erupted in anger. Letters poured in accusing Eleanor of trying to start a revolution. Wasn't she encouraging criminal behavior? How could she justify stealing? For a society to ensure "loyal and law abiding citizens," Eleanor explained, men like the one in her story needed to be given work. "Revolutions do not start until great groups of people are suffering and convinced of the hopelessness of their cause getting a fair hearing."

Eleanor weathered the furor with resolve. She didn't equivocate or back down from her vision—a world where no man or woman's family would go hungry again. "You do your best to make others see your point of view," she wrote, "but if you cannot win them over, you still must go on your way because each human being has an obligation to do what seems right according to his own conscience."

This kind of thinking had given Eleanor a public identity that rivaled her husband's as his first term swept toward his second. She seemed always to be in the thick of controversial issues and important administration decisions. She didn't hesitate to speak her mind clearly, passionately, and sometimes provocatively. Women should stop buying clothes from manufacturers who don't provide their workers with decent conditions, she argued. Child labor had to be ended, she pleaded. She denounced isolationism and reminded the reporters who attended her press conferences of the fears of war overseas. One day, Eleanor invited young African American girls from a nearby reform school to a garden party at the White House. Steve Early, the president's press secretary and a conservative southerner, blew up over the event, worried that Southern Democrats would be offended. They were, and the Southern newspapers picked up the outrage of the segregationists. By the time of the 1936 presidential campaign, cousin Alice Roosevelt Longworth wrote an article that sneered if "we didn't elect [Eleanor], what is she horning in for?"

Eleanor defied convention, and invited ridicule by reaching out to ordinary Americans as no first lady had done before. She believed that isolation and exclusion led to ignorance. She wanted to learn firsthand—not through aides' reports or by reading newspapers—about the issues that concerned her. To do this she traveled well outside the confines of Washington. She met with ordinary Americans, sitting in their homes, visiting their workplaces, even donning a hard hat and going down into a coal mine. She wanted to understand Americans' lives on a personal level. After seeing George Bernard Shaw's play *Saint Joan*, she remarked on the priest's line, "I did not know until I saw." To her, Shaw's words were "as true today as . . . when people were tortured and burned at the stake." She found meaning in the words, and she thought others should as well.

Sometimes the comments and stories about Eleanor's travels were humorous. She laughingly told of the man who had named his clock "Eleanor" because it was "always on the go." She chuckled over the tale that famed explorer Admiral Byrd set two places for dinner at the South Pole "just in case Mrs. Roosevelt should drop in." Sometimes even Franklin had trouble keeping track of his wife. One day he asked an usher to take a visitor to see her only to be told, "Mr. President, Mrs. Roosevelt has been out of town three days." An anonymous wag gave her the nickname "Eleanor Everywhere." She was called "ubiquitous," and it wasn't intended as a compliment.

Like Eleanor, every leader encounters criticism, justified or not. Sometimes it's easy to shake off, but often it can be cutting and even debilitating. Eleanor believed we all face two kinds of criticism: destructive and constructive. "To be really constructive, criticism must come to us from people whom we know and whose judgment we trust and who we feel really care, not only for us as individuals, but for the things which may be affected by the actions or attitudes which we take," Eleanor wrote. "Destructive criticism is always valueless and anyone with common sense soon becomes completely indifferent to it."

Eleanor's words imply a learning process. It takes time and thought to consider the kind of criticism you receive, and to deal with it in ways that at best enhance your leadership, and at worst stop short of damaging it. But, as Eleanor liked to say, "A woman is like a tea bag. You never know how strong she is until she gets in hot water."

*G*et Firsthand Information

The best defense against criticism is a good offense. If, like Eleanor, you gain a deep understanding of the issues you care about, you will be better able to handle obstacles to your goals. If you reach out to understand the concerns and dreams of those you hope to lead, you will be a more powerful leader. You can only do this by asking questions and listening, by reaching out to others and being open to them. You can't lead by staying behind your desk any more than Eleanor could lead by staying in the White House.

Gaining firsthand knowledge builds your confidence and effectiveness. It also communicates to those around you that you are a person of substance and authenticity, a leader who *knows* and *shows* the way. In *The Leadership Challenge*, James Kouzes and Barry Posner describe leaders who inspire a shared vision. "To enlist people in a vision, leaders must know their constituents and speak their language. People must believe that leaders understand their needs and have their interests at heart. Only through an intimate knowledge of their dreams, their hopes, their aspirations, their visions, their values is the leader able to enlist support."

Anita Roddick, founder of the Body Shop chain, offers a spectacular example of corporate success built on a grand and unique vision and powered by a hands-on approach. From the company's start in 1976, Roddick held the unconventional view that she could have a profitable company *and* fulfill core values of social activism, particularly around social and environmental concerns. Today Body Shop stores are located in forty-nine countries and trade in twenty-five different languages for the natural ingredients used in the company's products. Despite the far-flung nature of the business she conceived, Roddick is a hands-on executive. Traveling from rainforests in South America to villages in Africa, she has built her business around seeing, touching, smelling, and understanding her ingredients, closely overseeing product development, and staying in touch with her people. She's noted for setting tough standards, while maintaining great loyalty from franchisees and staff. They're willing to give their loyalty to

Roddick because she has built her authority by being on the frontline of her business and in close touch with her people.

The literal traveling of Eleanor and Anita Roddick serves as a dramatic example for your figurative "travels" as a leader, whatever the nature of your work. The problems you need to solve or the issues that need creative action may be down the hall, on the next floor, or in a set of papers no one has bothered to review. Either way, the leadership demands are the same. You must be willing to see and investigate for yourself. You must be eager to seek out those concerned, listen, learn, and look from all sides before deciding on a plan of action. By being proactive, you'll build your personal power to lead. Of course, not everyone will be cooperative. Trust may be slow in coming, personal attacks may be used to thwart you —but if you retreat from building your personal knowledge and understanding, you won't have a reservoir of experience and information to support your leadership.

Elouise Cobell learned the importance of getting the facts for herself when she acted on her vision to bring economic independence to the Blackfeet Indian tribe in Montana. Cobell grew up on the reservation in a house without electricity or running water. She educated herself to be an accountant. Hired by her own tribe in 1976, she began to see clearly what many had suspected: The federal government had failed to pay billions of dollars owed for tribal lands. The deception had been going on since 1887 when the government decided that it would handle all leasing and sale of Indian land. The money was to be held in trust and given out to Indian families; instead, it had been diverted to other federal efforts, such as bailing out New York City during its financial crisis in 1975. In some cases, government neglect and incompetence accounted for the Blackfeet's losses.

Cobell began to ask questions. She faced derision by government officials trying to humiliate her and discourage her from her mission. Her mother told her not to stir up trouble. But she continued digging into the secrets of the past, meeting with anyone who could educate her or who could help. She shook up the status quo with her passionate desire to help her people. She kept building her knowledge of the complexities of years of financial misdealing. "I tried to get a handle on everything," Cobell told *Parade* magazine in 2001, when the magazine did a cover story based on her efforts to recover tribal assets.

When Cobell got nowhere with Bureau of Indian Affairs staff at the local level, she went to Washington, D.C., even attending a meeting with officials from the Office of Management and Budget at the White House. Finally she led her people to join a class-action suit against the government. The case grew to represent a half-million Native Americans—and they won with a court ruling in 2000 that lambasted the government for failing to live up to its promises. The plaintiffs stand to recover $10 billion or more as the court begins to determine exactly how much is owed.

Cobell succeeded in turning around a century of fraud by arming herself with an unshakable command of facts and an unwavering dedication to her mission. She became a leader for the economic salvation of her people by seeing and learning about the problem firsthand. In fact, in her case she had lived with the problem. Armed with information and outrage, she had found the courage to act and face her critics.

At a Democratic women's breakfast before the 1936 election, Secretary of Labor Frances Perkins brought the audience to its feet with her remarks about the first lady. "She has gone out courageously, in the face of unfavorable criticism," Perkins marveled, "not only to meet the people as a friend, but to use that contact to make of herself a channel through which the needs and hopes and desires of people could be carried to places where solutions could be found to their problems." Seeing, listening, learning, and taking action— these were the steps that gave Eleanor the courage to lead in the face of any opposition.

Don't Let Critics Get in Your Way

Programs aimed at helping the nation's young people were especially close to Eleanor's heart. She felt urgently concerned about the number of young people who were unemployed and drifting away from the bonds of civil society. They were an unfettered mass ripe for a revolt or destructive behavior. They couldn't afford to stay in college, couldn't find work, couldn't hide their anger and frustration. "I live in real terror when I think we may be losing this generation,"

Eleanor told the *New York Times*. "We have got to bring these young people into the active life of the community and make them feel that they are necessary."

Working with the head of the Civilian Conservation Corps, Harry Hopkins, Eleanor pushed Franklin to adopt a plan that would provide job skills and education loans for young people while developing their sense of commitment to their communities and, ultimately, to democracy. People were divided on the advisability of her scheme. Some saw worrisome elements of the Hitler Youth in the plan, seeing this as just a way to indoctrinate young people, as the German leader was doing. Other people thought a democratic alternative to the Nazi youth propaganda effort made sense. Franklin's advisers fretted over political fallout, and the president tried to limit the program to an extension of the CCC. Eleanor held firm. She countered her critics by lobbying and publicly advocating for an expansive effort. Thanks to her work, the National Youth Administration was born. Young people were given part-time work and training as Eleanor envisioned. "It was one of the occasions on which I was proud that the right thing was done regardless of political considerations," she exulted.

People with more traditional ideas of the role of first lady grew increasingly annoyed with Eleanor. She should "light somewhere and keep quiet," advised the editor of the *Detroit Free Press*. After four years of the New Deal, the Roosevelt administration had no shortage of critics, and Eleanor's activities made her a target nearly as large as the president. She was called "Madam President," and "Empress Eleanor." In a vicious parody based on Edgar Allan Poe's poem *The Raven*, Congressman John Steven McGroarty wrote,

> *. . . and there comes a painful sighing*
> *From a people slowly dying*
> *Of a secret lust for gore;*
> *From a hopeless Nation crying*
> *For a surcease and a stilling*
> *Of the sound of Eleanor,*
> *Of the wordy Eleanor,*
> *Of the boresome Eleanor,*
> *Of the quenchless Eleanor.*

Critics believed Eleanor controlled Franklin, and even White House assistant Grace Tully called her "a one-woman staff for the President." One story that circulated in 1936 appeared in a Greenville, South Carolina, newspaper. According to the article, an unidentified pastor was defending FDR's policies when a parishioner repeatedly interrupted with shouts of, "I don't like him." In frustration, the pastor said, "He depends on a higher power for guidance." This time the man shouted, "I don't like her either." Many local media sources in the South looked for every opportunity to criticize Eleanor because of her strong support for civil rights.

Eleanor came to expect the jokes and attacks. Few women, Adlai Stevenson remembered, "have ever been subjected to personal abuse as malicious and persistent. But never did she hide, run, wince, or lower her head." As long as the anger was directed at her, and not at Franklin because of her, she saw little reason to worry. "As time went by," she wrote, "I found that people no longer considered me a mouthpiece for my husband but realized that I had a point of view of my own with which he might not at all agree. Then I felt freer to state my views."

State them she did—through writing, speeches, on radio, in lectures, and on any subject at any time. Fighting for women, children, young adults and the poor drove Eleanor's agenda as First Lady. After overcoming early prejudices of her own, she also became a powerful advocate for civil rights. More than anything else she did, Eleanor's work to end lynching, her friendship with black leaders, and her simple acts of respect and kindness for blacks made her the target of vicious anger.

A simple event, captured in the famous picture (later put on a postage stamp) of Eleanor accepting a flower from a black child in a slum-clearance project in Detroit, fueled right-wing hysteria. The picture of the first lady bending her tall frame to the eye level of the little girl and reaching out with a smile was plastered on flyers with scurrilous captions. In 1935, the racist paper *Georgia Woman's World* put a full-page spread of the picture on its back page, accusing the White House of failing to draw a "color line." Felix Frankfurter, the Harvard Law School professor who had given legal advice to Franklin when he was governor of New York and who would later be his Supreme Court appointee, wrote to Eleanor to offer support. "I know it's the very law of your being so to act—and that makes it all the more a source of pride for the Nation."

Not everyone was proud of Eleanor. No one knew what she would do next or where she might end up. Even Franklin couldn't be sure, but he knew she would be deeply involved in whatever problem touched her heart, whatever the risk. That's why one story Eleanor tells in her autobiography carries a touch of both truth and humor. As she tells it, she had decided to visit a prison in Baltimore to look at the wartime salvage work being done by the prisoners. "In order to fit the trip into my schedule I had to leave the White House early without saying good morning to Franklin. On his way to the office, he called to Tommy (Eleanor's secretary, Miss Thompson) and asked where I was. 'She's in prison, Mr. President,' Tommy said. 'I'm not surprised,' said Franklin, 'But what for?'"

Eleanor took pride in acting on her beliefs, regardless of the consequences. "Do what you feel in your heart to be right," she counseled others. "You'll be criticized anyway. You'll be damned if you do and damned if you don't."

Eleanor knew that criticism could be a roadblock to success, or an opportunity to become more effective. "If you consider that you are being criticized by someone who is seeking knowledge and has an open mind, then you naturally feel you must try to meet that criticism," Eleanor advised. "But if you feel that the criticism is made out of sheer malice and that no amount of explanation will change a point of view which has nothing to do with the facts, then the best thing is to put it out of your mind entirely."

Dee Francken, headmistress at the prestigious North London Collegiate School in London, has had many occasions to test Eleanor's advice. With a thick shock of cropped white hair and a broad smile, Francken is a strong leader who has faced criticism from a loyal but highly independent staff of well-respected teachers and administrators.

Francken's leadership values include a deep commitment to open communications with students' parents. So, early on in her tenure as headmistress, she tried to add a section on report cards that would allow parents to write comments back to teachers before the term ended. Thinking it was an unremarkable change and one that had worked well elsewhere, she called her staff of twenty together and made the announcement. They went into open revolt. "I really misjudged the reaction," Francken lamented. "The staff was frightened of what parents' would say, and of course, the naysayers shouted the loudest."

Francken listened, but told them they had to make the change. "The thing is not to crumble," she says, "but to give your critics a fair hearing and really listen to their concerns. I try to explain why I am dedicated to doing certain things, that we all have to take some chances and that nothing is written in concrete—we can always reconsider." But Francken also learned from the report card dust up. She established a small management team to help her screen new ideas and changes.

"It always helps to pick other peoples' brains, and they serve as my devil's advocates so I'm not blind-sided by critics later on."

Like Dee Francken and Eleanor, you can take control of situations that may open you up for criticism. You may feel insecure and question your choices, especially when you're under the gun, but you don't need to back down. Eleanor listened to her critics, sometimes she learned from them, but she never let them stop her if she felt she was right.

You can allow attacks to exaggerate, inflate, and inflame your worst view of yourself, but you can also choose to see attacks as an opportunity to reevaluate your course. Perhaps you'll make some changes, perhaps your best instincts will be reinforced. Either way, you will have maintained your control and power over the situation rather than losing faith in yourself. As Eleanor said, "No one can make you feel inferior without your consent."

*S*tay True to Yourself

When Eleanor counseled women to "develop a skin as thick as a rhinoceros hide," she was using colorful language to reinforce a simple idea: Protect who you are. Eleanor took many years to fully develop her passion and beliefs, but once she did she stayed true to herself. Her critics often asked why Eleanor couldn't "stay home with her husband and tend to her knitting as an example for other women to follow." But to Eleanor, traditions had been more trap than comfort. While she happened to enjoy knitting, and honored homely virtues with an array of family traditions, she was anything but traditional. Eleanor believed that women's leadership would come from women acting "on their own ability, on their own character as persons. Insincerity and sham, whether in men or in women, always fail in the end in public life." "Because she stood her ground," noted psychologist and author Howard Gardner, "she ended up enlarging the public's notions of what a woman could achieve on the American political scene."

Eleanor's actions on behalf of civil rights are just one example of how being true to herself led to dramatic social change. In the span of a few weeks in 1939, Eleanor became embroiled in two emotionally charged and very public racial situations. The first incident involved her attendance at the founding meeting of the Southern Conference on Human Welfare in Birmingham, Alabama. Blacks and whites were attending the meeting, but according to the city's segregation ordinance, they couldn't sit together. City officials threatened to shut down the conference if the ordinance wasn't followed. When Eleanor entered the hall, she walked to the front and sat on the black side of the center aisle. The police quickly approached and told the first lady she was violating the law. Eleanor had her chair moved to the aisle between the two sides, and there she sat throughout the meeting.

Her confounding defiance of Birmingham's segregationist practices caught national attention. Most black

Americans and antisegregationists considered her action heroic. Certainly she could have taken an easier course. She could have moved to the white side of the room and argued that she didn't want to cause a disruption at the meeting. Had she chosen this approach, her reserve of goodwill in the black community would probably have shielded her from criticism. But Eleanor acted out of conviction.

Within weeks of the incident in Birmingham, the first lady found herself confronting another issue of conscience. Marian Anderson, the greatest living contralto of her time, was African American. In 1939, Anderson stood at the peak of her career, having traveled throughout Europe performing for heads of state. She had entertained the Roosevelts at the White House and formed a warm friendship with Eleanor.

In January 1939, Howard University invited Anderson to perform in Washington, D.C., on Easter Sunday. They tried to rent the largest site in the city, Constitution Hall in the grand building owned by the Daughters of the American Revolution, but the organization refused. Seven years before, the DAR had adopted a rule barring African Americans from performing in Constitution Hall because of protests over racially mixed seating during performances by black artists.

People were outraged at the DAR's decision and protests began flowing in from around the country. Eleanor was equally appalled, particularly because of her longtime membership in the organization. Although Eleanor had often worked for change from the inside when she disagreed with an organization's decisions, in this case the issue had become too public for her to work quietly for reform. "I am in complete disagreement with the attitude taken in refusing Constitution Hall to a great artist," she wrote to the DAR president. "You have set an example which seems to me unfortunate, and I feel obliged to send in to you my resignation. You had an opportunity to lead in an enlightened way and it seems to me that your organization has failed."

Eleanor's resignation turned the episode into an event that attracted worldwide news, and the public rallied behind her. A Gallup poll showed overwhelming support for her stand. Friends and strangers wrote to praise her. But Eleanor wasn't finished. Working with Interior Secretary Harold Ickes, she helped arrange a new venue for Anderson's concert. On a chilly Easter Sunday, Marian Anderson stood on the steps of the Lincoln Memorial in front of a cheering crowd of 75,000 people. Anderson looked majestic in her beaded dress and fur coat. The singer felt overwhelmed and, for a moment, unsure of her voice. Then she began singing "God Bless America," and the music swelled over the crowd with thrilling intensity. The one person who didn't hear the concert, however, was Eleanor. She chose to give her friend Marian Anderson the full spotlight.

Eleanor's action on behalf of Anderson drew Republican attacks during her husband's 1940 reelection bid, but it also caused millions to think of her as a hero. As writer Vernon Jarrett remembered, "Most black people were struck with the genuineness and the feeling that she was for real, not only just her statements, not only the so-called sympathetic statements. Her statements were empathetic rather than sympathetic. She showed empathy."

In ways large and small, Eleanor weighed her choices based on a clear understanding of what she stood for and who she was. She didn't let others shape her opinion of herself or dislodge her understanding of events. You can do the same by choosing to overcome setbacks and work through objections.

Francine Dellabadia learned this lesson as a divisional vice president for women's merchandising at the corporate office of a high-end manufacturer of leather goods and accessories. A willowy thirty-two-year-old with large brown eyes, Francine is in charge of a top-level team that works on product strategies.

"Criticism isn't something that can be predicted or prevented," Dellabadia says. "In today's world you just have to be true to yourself, because sometimes people are trying to get you to change things that you believe are essential to your success. You have to remember that those criticizing you have their own issues, and you have to get past those to assess whether their comments have any validity."

Finding the courage to be a strong leader is a quest. It will take you into new areas of learning. It will bring you new relationships and new understandings of people and the world. It will teach you that you can't please all the people, but that you have to please yourself.

ELEANOR'S WAY

- Build your firsthand knowledge around the issues and ideas where you want to take leadership. Don't be desk-bound.

- Reach out to people. Listen and learn about their concerns.

- Develop your knowledge so that you're prepared for your critics.

- Be a leader who knows the way before she shows the way.

- Understand that with leadership comes criticism. Expect it and be ready for it.

- Distinguish between criticism that you value and can use versus criticism that is best ignored.

- Handle criticism with less emotion and more intelligence. Be open to constructive ideas. Be strong in the face of unjust attacks.

- Test your ideas on a small group before going public, and be ready to make adjustments based on feedback.

- Stay true to your values and vision. Don't let others impose a role on you or ascribe negative behaviors to you that really reflect their own issues.

- Keep working on your understanding of yourself and lead according to your own beliefs and values.

CHAPTER NINE

Keep Your Focus

*"To be useful is, in a way,
to justify one's own existence.
The difficult thing, perhaps, is
to learn how to be useful,
to recognize needs
and to attempt to meet them."*
—ER

*E*veryone in Washington felt the quickening pulse of the coming war in Europe as the 1930s drew to a close. The fascism that fueled aggression overseas had ugly parallels in the United States. Anti-Semitism and racism reached a fever pitch of twisted patriotism. Communists were equated with Jews, and both were accused of plotting to overthrow the American government. Zealots circulated a chart in the shape of a Star of David, showing Jewish appointments in Roosevelt's administration, with the title "Roosevelt's Supreme Council."

In 1939, Eleanor's longtime colleague and friend, Labor Secretary Frances Perkins, found herself before the Judiciary Committee on a resolution of impeachment. Her offense: refusal to deport the labor leader Harry Bridges, an alleged Communist. Enterprising slanderers, eager to discredit Perkins, started a national whisper campaign, claiming that Perkins had hidden her Jewish ancestry. Perkins, a Yankee brought up in the Congregational Church, was forced into a public denial, but added, "if I were a Jew . . . I'd be proud to acknowledge it."

Eleanor worried about the effects of the unreasoning fear that whipped so many people into a frenzy of hatred. "People have reached a point where anything which will save them from Communism is a godsend; and if Fascism or Nazism promises more security than our own democracy we may even turn to them," she wrote with concern in early 1939.

Suddenly, the war in Europe hit full stride, keeping White House lights burning far into the night. German troops erased the border with Poland, swiftly marching into the country on September 1, 1939. Eight months later, Hitler invaded Denmark, attacked Norway, and threw out the British troops that fought back. The next month, May 1940, Hitler charged into Belgium, Holland, and Luxembourg, all neutral countries, and began his offensive into the north of France. Italy quickly attacked the French from the south.

Eleanor loathed the idea of another war after her experiences in World War I. She had thrown herself into war work in 1918 with long hours in the army canteens and wrenching visits to the wounded. She had visited the battlefields after the war and seen the devastation up close. In the late summer of 1939 she wrote in her "My Day" column, "Let's ask our leaders not to weaken their stand against war, but to tell us what more could be done for permanent peace." She was dubbed "America's Number One Pacifist." With four grown sons ready to serve their country and her husband as commander in chief, she had personal as well as deeply held moral reasons for wishing that war could be avoided. But it could not, and Eleanor, the "realistic pacifist," was soon drawn into the war effort.

In the midst of Hitler's military escalation and intense isolationist sentiment in America, FDR had to decide whether to seek a third term. Even Eleanor, who had never been anxious to stay in Washington, understood the need for his continued leadership. Refusing even to attend the Democratic convention in Chicago, FDR nevertheless became his party's unanimous choice for the 1940 race. Still, when he chose Henry Wallace as a running mate, the convention balked. FDR threatened to pull out if the delegates didn't approve Wallace, then asked Eleanor to speak to the delegates on his behalf, an unprecedented action for a first lady.

Eleanor sensed that FDR had a special reason for choosing Wallace. The president knew his health could be severely strained by a third term. As a stalwart liberal in FDR's cabinet, Wallace was someone FDR trusted to carry forward the New Deal agenda if the president failed to finish his term. Eleanor agreed to fly to Chicago, a single carry-bag in her hand.

Pandemonium reigned in the convention hall, but according to press accounts, "the tumult of 50,000" stilled when Eleanor began to speak. Why did she command such respect from the fractious delegates? Why were they willing to listen to this woman who held no office and had no formal authority? Perhaps it was because she spoke for the president, but there was something more.

More women stood on the convention floor because Eleanor had spent nearly two decades fighting to increase their numbers. She had sat outside the closed-door meetings of the men in charge of the Party in the 1920s, waiting for hours to argue the case for greater representation by women. When they refused she came back again and again, and she brought other women with her. Now, in 1940, women delegates in the hall were grateful for the ground she had broken as a different kind of first lady.

Even among her detractors, especially those Democrats who thought she hurt the president politically with her activism, there was grudging respect. Although no one had voted for Eleanor, the measure of her influence stood in stacks on her desk—thousands of letters from ordinary Americans who looked to her for inspiration and help. She answered those letters, sometimes by staying up through the night. Like every leader, she understood the importance of letting her followers know that she heard them, cared about them, and would act on their behalf.

She had also strengthened the party by bringing in blacks who for generations had voted for the party of Lincoln, the Republicans. But Eleanor showed up at black churches and organization meetings, she invited black leaders to the White House to talk about civil rights, she advocated tirelessly on their behalf. Historian Allida Black wrote, "ER's commitment to racial justice was both so public and so routine that her name became synonymous with early demands for civil rights." Eleanor had led black Americans to the Democratic Party, and their allegiance would remain with the party for the rest of the century.

So as she stood before the delegates, their faces turned with expectation and respect toward the podium. She struck a simple theme, speaking without notes. She called on them to follow a higher purpose than mere party infighting, emphasizing that whoever became president took on "a heavier responsibility, perhaps, than any man has ever faced before in this country." Tall and erect, her beautiful thick hair now tinged with gray, she admonished the delegates. "You will have to rise above considerations which are narrow and partisan. This is a time when it is the United States we fight for."

Back in Hyde Park, Franklin listened with approval. He hadn't told her what to say; he had trusted that she would know. He had learned, as the nation had learned, that Eleanor led by asking people to be better, to do better. She could have argued Wallace's qualifications or threatened the delegates with FDR's withdrawal; instead, she appealed to principle, asking them to act as patriots. They followed her call and Wallace won the nomination for vice president.

On election night, as returns confirmed Roosevelt's victory over Wendell Willkie, Eleanor called on the nation to work together as U.S. involvement in the war in Europe seemed more and more inevitable. "May what is best for the country happen today, and may we all remember that whatever happens, this is just the beginning of some years of useful work," she wrote in her column.

But Eleanor worried over what her "useful work" would be. FDR's focus on the growing war threat would drain resources and attention from the issues she had worked on since 1933. She had done a masterful job in ensuring her husband the presidency on his terms, but her usefulness to him and the nation seemed over. In a moment of insecurity, she confided to her daughter Anna that living in the White House "is very oppressive . . . . What you think or feel seems of no use or value . . . ." FDR announced that he had changed from "Dr. New Deal," to "Dr. Win-the-War," but in a country preparing for war, what leadership title could Eleanor claim?

Flexibility and Focus

Leaders are able to show flexibility, to change with circumstances while continuing to move toward their larger vision. They do it by looking for opportunity and avoiding distraction. Eleanor counseled patience and courage, offering the perfect approach for adjusting personal vision as one's status or situation changes. "We do not have to become heroes overnight," she wrote, "Just a step at a time, meeting each thing that comes up, seeing it is not as dreadful as it appears, discovering that we have the strength to stare it down." Eleanor's powerful sense of responsibility propelled her to go a step further. "You must do the thing you think you cannot do," Eleanor wrote with conviction born from a lifetime of experience.

When the war threatened to push Eleanor's priorities to the background, she found a new way to make change. If questions of military housing were raised, she broadened the debate to include housing for the homeless and badly sheltered. If the ill health of military recruits came up, she raised the issue of national health care. In this way she began to weave the unfinished business of the New Deal into the issues of the new war-obsessed administration. Looking back, Eleanor explained in her autobiography, "It was the New Deal social objectives that had fostered the spirit that would make it possible for us to fight the war, and I believed it was vastly important to give people the feeling that in fighting the war we were still really fighting for these same objectives."

Eleanor kept the New Deal alive during the war because she believed that its programs were essential to the health of the democracy. According to historian Doris Kearns Goodwin, Eleanor repeatedly said that "unless democracy were renewed at home . . . there was little merit in fighting for democracy abroad." Without Eleanor's advocacy, Goodwin continues, "the tendency to put first things first, to focus on winning the war before exerting effort on anything else, might well have prevailed."

All of us have times when we face a seemingly insurmountable future or impossible choice. I did when I was in my late twenties. Unhappy with my career in education, I thought about going to law school. I had no money saved, no one to pay the tuition, and grave doubts that I was disciplined enough to get through the rigorous course work after being out of school for a while. I took the entrance exam and wrote two applications anyway.

Suddenly, my life changed dramatically. I got an acceptance letter from a law school the same week that I received an offer to take the education director's job at a large organization. The job represented a big promotion, but law school fit my passion for advocacy and my vision of fighting for women's rights. The job choice was safe and secure; law school in a big city where I didn't know anyone seemed impossible.

I decided to go for the impossible. I sold my car for a down payment on tuition. I took a job shopping and cooking for a wealthy couple, both lawyers, in exchange for living in the servant's quarters of their posh apartment near my law school. I studied late into the night and often doubted that I would make it to graduation. But I renewed my determination by looking at a gift a friend had given me when I left for school—a bronze nameplate set on a block of wood, the kind a lawyer would have on her desk, with ROBIN GERBER, ESQ. engraved on it. That gift still serves as a reminder for me that trying the impossible is often the very best thing to do.

Think Long, Think Transformation

To stay focused on her vision during the war years, Eleanor looked ahead past wartime, linking her vision to values of patriotism and democracy. Eleanor envisioned a better nation after the war, a country with more shared wealth and less divisive injustice. With this long view in mind, she began to work on immediate concerns.

Eleanor warned FDR that Congress was trying to cut out food stamp and school lunch programs and urged him to save them. To back up her position, she cited data that nearly 40 percent of the first million men drafted were found unfit to serve. For many of them, poor nutrition accounted for poor health. This showed the need not only to continue the food programs, but also to teach about nutrition, and start a national health care system, Eleanor argued.

She lobbied within the administration, but she didn't stop there. She also kept track of the twists and legislative turns of the issues she cared about, calling agency heads or administration insiders whenever she needed more information. Her years of work to place women in positions of influence in government paid off by giving her rich sources of information and early warnings of attacks on programs she cared about. She used this information to communicate with her audience—the American people—through her column and other means. Her overtures were not always welcome, but she was persistent.

When it came to lobbying Franklin on issues she felt strongly about, Eleanor held powerful sway. According to Rexford Tugwell, a close adviser to FDR, "No one who ever saw Eleanor Roosevelt sit down facing her husband and holding his eyes firmly [saying] to him, 'Franklin, I think that you should . . .' or 'Franklin, surely you will note . . .' will ever forget the experience. It would be impossible to say how often and to what extent American governmental processes have been turned in a new direction because of her determination," Tugwell concluded.

Eleanor also used the president's cabinet to advance her causes. Interior Secretary Harold Ickes ran the Public Works Administration, a New Deal program that put government money behind job-creating projects across the country. The PWA had a cumbersome approval process for projects. If Eleanor heard about an area in dire need, she didn't hesitate to call Ickes to get him to speed things up. When one of Eleanor's assistants sent her a newspaper clipping about the languishing Detroit Slum Clearance Project, she quickly sent a note to Ickes and broke the logjam. Ickes often shared Eleanor's concerns, but he could find her meddlesome, especially when she went around him in his own department. "Soon I will expect Sistie and Buzzy (Eleanor's grandchildren) to be issuing orders to members of my staff," Ickes wrote in his diary. "Fortunately they can't write yet."

Sometimes Eleanor's efforts in pursuit of her vision brought her into conflict with FDR. This happened in 1940 as Congress struggled over the question of the draft. The army and navy were pushing for military service and a one-year commitment, but Eleanor had more expansive ideas, ideas that her husband never endorsed.

"National defense means more than military training. It means the building up of physique, of character, and of a people conscious of what they owe to their country," she announced at a press conference. Eleanor wanted everyone drafted and given a job for the war effort, some in the military abroad, others right on American soil. In her national service, everyone would learn useful skills, become physically fit, and help to rebuild decaying communities.

Eleanor didn't just see the draft as a chance to train young men for battle; she saw the opportunity to train an entire nation—men and women—for democracy. Looking beyond the immediate needs of the war, Eleanor envisioned a postwar nation strengthened by common effort and sacrifice by all.

FDR and his advisers weren't buying Eleanor's plan. They feared stirring up isolationist sentiment by combining reform with defense. They were afraid of alienating certain businesspeople who were needed to push war production. As an example of transactional leadership, put forward by leadership scholar James MacGregor Burns, FDR was most comfortable as the horse trader, giving and taking, based on short-term needs and goals.

As FDR effected change by transacting, Eleanor was busy transforming, Burns says. "The transforming leader looks for potential motives in followers, seeks to satisfy higher needs, and engages the full person of the follower," Burns writes.

"The result of transforming leadership is a relationship of mutual stimulation and elevation that converts followers into leaders and may convert leaders into moral agents."

Eleanor emerged in wartime as a transforming leader and moral agent, undeterred by setbacks. Even though her national conscription idea didn't get passed into law, she kept trying. She brought a version of the plan to the job she held in the Office of Civil Defense. According to Eleanor, civil defense meant, "the participation of every individual throughout the country in a volunteer job who is able to do so." Further, the volunteer jobs should be "useful to the communities." Unfortunately, Eleanor discovered what First Lady Hillary Clinton learned fifty years later: A president's wife is too much of a target to hold a position in her husband's administration. Eleanor's critics claimed she had appointed radicals and Communists and hired her friends, giving them large salaries. Half-truths were turned into scandal. Under attack, Eleanor chose to leave the OCD job shortly after the Japanese bombed Pearl Harbor and before her national service plan could be implemented.

Like all leaders of vision, setbacks in moving her dreams forward didn't stop Eleanor from trying again. As World War II drew to a close she again raised the idea of a mandatory year of national service for young men and women. "Our youngsters must get it into their minds that they have a responsibility to their country," she wrote.

It would be decades after the war before the Peace Corps, AmeriCorps, Senior Corps, and high school commu-

ER with troops in Central and South America, 1944.

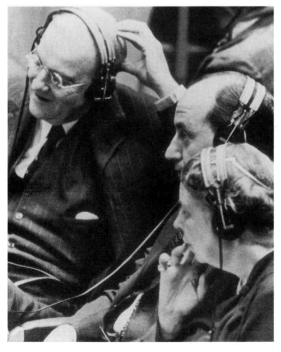

John Foster
Dulles, Adlai
Stevenson, and ER
at a UN session,
1946.

ER and Harry
Truman at
Hyde Park,
1946.

Eleanor Roosevelt with reporters Emma Bugbee, Doroth Ducas, Ruby
Black, and Bess Furman in Puerto Rico, 1934.

ER with Marian Anderson in Japan, 1953.

ER and Mrs. Winston Churchill at a Canadian conference, 1944.

ER and Frank Sinatra talking at a dinner, 1947.

ER in Bombay, India, 1952.

ER in Israel, 1959.

ER on *Meet the Press,* 1956.

ER and Fala at Val-Kill, 1948.

ER cooking at Val-Kill, 1938.

ER head shot at a UN meeting in Paris, 1951.

ER and the Universal Declaration of Human Rights printed in Spanish, 1949.

ER and Mary McLeod Bethune, 1960.

ER, 1960.

ER and JFK in Waltham Mass., 1960.

Kennedy, Johnson, Truman, and Eisenhower at ER's funeral, 1962.

nity service requirements all came about. But Eleanor didn't expect immediate results from the idea of mandatory national service or any of her other transforming ideas. She intended to "interest people and bring about discussion." She led by being a catalyst for change, and created an environment where followers became leaders as they were drawn into her stories and motivated to act by her vision.

People who heard Eleanor speak quoted her long afterward. They debated her ideas, wrote letters to her and to editorial pages about her. Some were flattering, some not, but Eleanor had achieved her goal of getting America talking and thinking about big, important new ideas.

Of course, as first lady, Eleanor had a privileged chance to bring her vision to the national stage. Can transforming leadership be translated to your workplace? Do you hold a transforming vision for your work? Cindy Hallberlin did when she served as an attorney for the U.S. Postal Service in the 1990s.

Hallberlin had spent more than a decade defending the Postal Service against charges of discrimination under Title VII of the Civil Rights Act. Repeatedly, she observed employees who had legitimate grievances, but who were ill served by the drawn-out and contentious process involved in the claims. Whether employees or the Postal Service won the cases, renewed complaints, disciplinary problems, poor morale, and frustration continued on both sides. The cases drained enormous amounts of revenue and staff time from the Postal Service's main mission of delivering the nation's mail.

One day Hallberlin was assigned to a ten-year-old class action case that had no end in sight. Appalled at the situation, she convinced the opposing attorney to agree to try a new remedy—mediation. No one in the Postal Service, the nation's largest employer at the time, had ever done that before. She found the seed of a transforming idea built on her belief that "you can't just throw money at the problem, you have to look at different solutions."

Hallberlin then proposed a national conflict resolution plan that would divert cases heading for litigation into a mediation process. Cases would move faster, time and money would be saved, and the Postal Service would set a standard for a less litigious society. "The hard part was moving the institution to go from a win-lose mentality to a win-win process where the goal was not just to win cases but to improve the workplace climate and culture," Hallberlin explained. "The whole mentality was [that of] gladiators, not people. Everybody thought I'd fail."

They seemed to be right. When Hallberlin first asked to set up a mediation division, she hit a wall. "Management told me no money, no beef, no nothing—you have no data. So I said we'll study the hell out of it and come back with data. Nobody believed I could come back with so much, but I did." She only had one assistant, but together they canvassed the country devising a questionnaire to gather information. If they didn't get responses, Hallberlin followed up with calls until she did.

A major shift in policy, procedure, and culture does not happen easily anywhere, much less within a workplace with more than 850,000 employees. Forming and implementing the idea took Hallberlin three and a half years of facing the naysayers and adjusting to shifting political ground. But the final report she put together to launch the project was finished at the perfect time. The Government Accounting Office had just charged the Postal Service with horrible labor relations for the second time. Congress held hearings and bristled over the steep increase in Postal Service employee discrimination complaints and the backlog of more than 100,000 grievances. The postmaster needed to point to some effort at change. Hallberlin took advantage of the moment and pressed forward with her mediation vision. "Politically [the mediation plan] would never have flown if it weren't for the congressional oversight," she said.

Hallberlin's vision included not only resolving equal employment opportunity complaints, but also building communication skills between workers and management and giving them more control over the process. She hit on the idea of using a method called "transformative mediation." With a two-year budget of $22 million and 105 new full-time positions, Hallberlin started a nationwide training program in the transformative method for outside mediators as well as postal employees. She put more than four thousand supervisors, managers, and union officials through a one-day conflict management course, and she began resolving cases through mediation instead of litigation.

Hallberlin's vision was credited with revolutionizing how the Postal Service manages conflict as well as influencing organizations in both the public and private sector. Today, as an attorney at a prominent nationwide law firm, Hallberlin is extending her transformative mediation vision to corporations and governments all over the world.

Like Eleanor, Cindy Hallberlin used her experience to create a transforming vision, and to act as a transforming leader. In *Women on Power: Leadership Redefined* author Susan Freeman articulates the kind of traits Hallberlin displayed. "Transformational leadership," Freeman writes, "is characterized . . . by integrity, honesty, trustworthiness, team orientation, decisiveness, intelligence, and win-win problem solving."

For Eleanor, building leadership in others was at the heart of lasting change. "I think I am right when I say that it is not just enough to give people who have suffered a better house and better wages," Eleanor told the National Urban League in 1936. "You must give them education and understanding and training before you can expect them to take up their full responsibility." As leadership scholar Bernard Bass has written, leadership in organizations means inspiring followers to increase their efforts and their successes.

Your job as a transforming leader is to develop a clear, strong vision, to be determined and persistent, and to build leadership in those around you. If you do, you'll find that you can make great changes, achieve maximum success, and leave a lasting legacy as a transforming leader.

The Power of Conviction

There may be no more powerful way to stay focused than to believe strongly in your goals. Eleanor's conviction in the causes that she espoused was clear. One notorious case involved Odell Waller, a twenty-three-year-old black sharecropper who went to claim his share of a wheat crop from his white landlord on July 15, 1940 in Pittsylvania, Virginia. He ended up on trial for shooting the landlord to death. The jury of white landowners convicted him, but civil rights groups challenged the verdict, arguing that Waller did not have a jury of his peers. Not surprisingly, as the case grew into a national referendum on class and racial justice, black leaders appealed to Eleanor for help.

As biographer and close friend Joseph Lash wrote, "There was little that the Negro people demanded of their government that did not end up as an appeal to her." Eleanor threw herself into the Waller case. She pleaded with the president to intervene with the governor of Virginia to commute the death sentence to life in prison. She argued with FDR and his top aide, Harry Hopkins, "to the point of exasperation." For Eleanor, there was no other way. "Every time we shirk making up our minds or standing up for a cause in which we believe," she wrote, "we weaken our character and our ability to be fearless."

Eleanor finally got Franklin to make a call. It didn't help. She wrote and called the governor herself. She gave money and advice for Waller's defense. "My Day" became a forum to argue the case to the nation. As the date for the execution approached, Eleanor refused to take no for an answer, even when FDR refused to take her repeated calls. When he finally gave in, he told her that under no circumstances would he put more pressure on the Virginia governor. In a sorrowful call, Eleanor told Waller supporters, "I have done everything I can possibly do."

On the day before Waller was electrocuted, Harry Hopkins wrote a memorandum about Eleanor's appeals. "This incident is typical of the things that have gone on in Washington between the President and Mrs. Roosevelt ever since 1932. She is forever finding someone underprivileged and unbefriended in whose behalf she takes up the cudgels. While she may often be wrong . . . I never cease to admire her burning determination to see that justice is done, not only to individuals, but to underprivileged groups."

Hopkins was right, at least about the extent of Eleanor's efforts. At the same time that she fought to save Odell Waller's life, she fought on a second, bigger, and more volatile front. Black Americans were being systematically refused the opportunity to serve in the armed forces. The military buildup that began in 1940 drew thousands of hopeful black recruits who quickly discovered that they were headed for segregated units if they were accepted at all. "I know how bitterly the Negro people are disturbed over their inability to participate in national defense or to obtain employment in defense industries," Eleanor wrote in her "My Day" column on June 18, 1941.

The ban on enlistment kept the regular army 90 percent white. There were no black marines or army pilots, and only one of a total of four black units was given combat training. In the entire army there were only two black officers. With Secretary of War Henry Stimson stating that "leadership is not embedded in the Negro race yet," it was not surprising that blacks in the navy were treated like service workers on the sea, confined to jobs like dishwashing and cleaning duties. As the nation moved to a war footing, the issue of black enlistment began to eclipse the focus by black leaders on antilynching laws.

Eleanor launched herself into the campaign for racial equality in the military with a speech to the Brotherhood of Sleeping Car Porters in 1940. The charismatic founder of the union, A. Phillip Randolph, took the opportunity to tell Eleanor that he and Eleanor's friend, NAACP leader Walter White, had been trying to arrange a meeting with the president on the conscription problem. The new draft law gave lip service to increasing racial equality in the military, but there were loopholes that needed to be closed. Could Eleanor help them get the president's ear?

That night Eleanor wrote to her husband. When she returned to Washington she talked to FDR directly. He knew how tenacious she could be. "When you take a position on an issue your backbone has no bend!" he had once complained.

Within weeks, much to the chagrin of the president's aides, Eleanor arranged for Randolph and White to meet with the navy secretary, the assistant secretary of war, and the president. Randolph, White, and Arnold Hill from the Urban League laid out a plan for bringing blacks in as officers, doctors, dentists, and other specialists, providing them with aviation training, hiring them as civilians in defense departments, and making other changes to remedy the racial imbalance. The president listened, and things seemed to go well. Then presidential press secretary Steve Early mistakenly announced that Randolph, White, and Hill had caved in on a policy that would continue segregation.

Walter White and the others exploded in anger. Eleanor intervened with Franklin who apologized for the misstatement. But the damage couldn't be easily contained. Furious letters poured into the White House and mass meetings were held. White House concern grew over losing the black vote in an election year. Battling to contain the political damage, FDR promoted a black colonel to brigadier general and appointed a prominent black civilian to the War Department. Throughout the controversy, Eleanor remained the "in-house" advocate, recognizing with satisfaction that the ball she had started rolling with the initial meeting at the White House had gathered great weight.

Eleanor fought on other civil rights fronts as well. She battled against the defense industry's exclusion of blacks from domestic jobs. She fought the segregationist Jim Crow system that had imbedded itself in the military resulting in unequal recreation facilities and other services for African Americans in the military.

Eleanor brought the same conviction and dogged determination to women's rights issues that she brought to the civil rights struggle during the war. "Hers was a conscience combined with an almost demonic commitment and tenacity," wrote James MacGregor Burns. When the Japanese bombed Pearl Harbor in December 1941, Eleanor quickly and accurately predicted that women would be needed to work in war production factories. Drawing on the personal leadership style that the public had come to expect, Eleanor told a Boston newspaper, "I'm pretty old, 57 you know, to tell girls what to do with their lives, but if I were of a debutante age I would go into a factory—any factory where I could learn a skill and be useful." She urged the young women to go out and get "every bit of preparation they could to expand their horizons."

Women pulled on pants and poured into factories for war work. They drove trucks and ran heavy machinery with an energy and efficiency that took management by surprise. Plant managers began to beg for more female workers.

Eleanor reveled in visiting the plants and talking to women on the job. At the South Portland shipbuilding yard, she listened for two hours as women talked about loving their work and taking pride in it, but suffering on the home front. How could they care for children, feed their families, take care of the household, and still keep up their work? they fretted.

Traveling to Des Moines, Iowa, Eleanor found women had flooded into the newly formed Women's Army Auxiliary Corps to fill jobs as cooks, telephone operators, and airplane spotters. As always, Eleanor took a full tour, listening to the women talk of rising at five A.M. and scrubbing floors until their knees looked like balloons. Eleanor felt proud and worried. She saw that the plan for bringing women into the working world had given scant attention to the homes they left behind. She feared the whole system would collapse if the women weren't given more support. In 1942, Eleanor had successfully pressed Franklin into approving the first government-backed day care. But nearly two million children needed care and this first effort only covered 105,000. What of the others?

Eleanor decided to focus on private industry. Corporate leaders had to see day care as a service as integral to their operations as the company cafeteria. With six million women expected in the workforce before the war ended, the child care issue had to be addressed. Horror stories had begun to circulate. A woman working the midnight shift had reportedly left her children sleeping in the car. Young children were frequently being left unattended.

Eleanor went to the giant Kaiser shipyards in Portland, Oregon. Using all her persuasive might, she asked Kaiser executives to set up a model child-care center. The company had more than four thousand mothers working in the plants. Letting them bring their children to an on-site day care center could boost productivity, she argued.

Kaiser agreed to build a state-of-the-art facility called Swan Island. A fine staff ran an integrated center where white, Mexican, Indian, and black children played and learned together. Other war plants copied the successful experiment, and the idea of child care as a national concern took root in the public mind.

Eleanor's conviction around the rights and needs of women went well beyond child care. She suggested every-thing from community laundries to restaurants that would prepare meals for working women to pick up on their way home. Children should have transportation from home to school and back, she said. Personal shoppers should pack groceries for women workers so they wouldn't miss their chance to buy meat, which often was gone from stores by the time their shifts ended. Many working women today enjoy corporate perks that range from on-site day care to on-site dry cleaning. Conviction, the absolute belief in her vision, led Eleanor to creative solutions well ahead of her time.

How strongly do you believe in your vision? What is the depth of your conviction? Eleanor wrote, "Surely, in the light of history, it is more intelligent to hope rather than to fear, to try rather than not to try." Like Eleanor, focusing on your hopes will lead you to be a transforming leader.

ELEANOR'S WAY

- Remain true to your leadership passion even when you face drastically changed circumstances. You can adjust your vision to fit the times.

- Make a plan. Remember that you don't have to do everything all at once. Work one step at a time toward your vision, bringing people along as you go.

- Believe that you can do the impossible.

- Focus on the future. Take time to think about what may happen and how it fits your plans.

- Embrace change. See it as an opportunity not a setback. Be the person who steps up to the new challenge and brings others along.

- Use every avenue, every method, and every opportunity to advance your vision.

- Think in terms of transforming change—change that will have broad and long-lasting effect.

- Stay focused on your goals and be persistent in pursuing them.

- Build loyalty and a legacy to carry on transforming change by encouraging leadership in other people.

CHAPTER TEN

Contacts, Networks, and Connections

"Human relationships, like life itself, can never remain static."

—ER

*W*ith a large oval brooch at her throat and a simple tailored dress, Eleanor looked "unusually smart and in soaring spirits" on April 12, 1945. After giving her speech at a Washington, D.C., charity event, she sat listening to the tributes and musical entertainment that followed. But her demeanor was forced. Just before coming to the event she had been told that Franklin had fainted in Warm Springs, Georgia. Suddenly a messenger approached to whisper in her ear. She gave a quick start and went to the telephone. Press Secretary Steve Early was at the other end. He sounded "very much upset," according to Eleanor, asking her to come home at once. "I did not even ask why. I knew down in my heart that something dreadful had happened."

At the White House, Eleanor's fears were confirmed. Franklin had died of a cerebral hemorrhage that afternoon. She immediately sent for Vice President Truman. Then she cabled her sons overseas. Only a month earlier American soldiers had stormed into Germany bringing that country to the verge of surrender, but the war in the Pacific still raged, and the Roosevelt boys were all in uniform. "He did his job to the end as he would want you to do," their mother's cable read.

Eleanor had changed to a black dress by the time Truman arrived. She stepped toward him, raising her hand gently to his shoulder. "Harry, the president is dead." Truman stood stunned. "Is there anything I can do for you?" he finally said. "Is there anything *we* can do for *you*?" Eleanor replied. "For you are the one in trouble now."

After Truman was sworn in, Eleanor spent five hours traveling to the simple white cottage in Warm Springs where Franklin had come for many years to rest and treat his paralysis. Walking past the vine-covered porch pillars, Eleanor, looking calm and in control, went inside to embrace Franklin's secretary, Grace Tully, and his cousins Margaret Suckley and Laura Delano. Settling together on the sofa, Eleanor asked to hear about her husband's last hours.

He had been sitting for a portrait, signing documents, seemingly in good spirits, according to Tully and Suckley. Then came Laura Delano's turn. The eccentric aristocrat spoke with blunt cruelty. The portrait was being painted by Elizabeth Shoumatoff, a friend of Lucy Mercer Rutherford, she told Eleanor. Rutherford, married and widowed since her affair with Franklin, had been visiting for several days, Delano went on. In fact, she had been sitting in the window seat when Franklin collapsed.

Visibly shocked, Eleanor struggled to control herself. More than a quarter century had passed since she first learned of her husband's affair. To save his marriage to Eleanor, he had promised to never see Lucy Mercer again. No one can know what Eleanor felt as she rose and went to the bedroom where Franklin's body lay. In five minutes she came out looking solemn, her eyes dry.

The next day she rode on the funeral train as it slowly traveled toward Washington. Lying in her berth through the long night, Eleanor looked out and remembered her husband. She wrote later about gazing "at the countryside he had loved . . . watching the faces of the people at stations, and even at the crossroads, who came to pay their last tribute all through the night."

Eleanor quickly moved forward with her changed life. The Trumans offered to let her stay in the White House as long as she wanted, but she refused, moving to her apartment in New York a week later. She thought of herself as being on her own. She wrote in her autobiography, "I had to face the future as countless other women have faced it without their husbands."

But in at least one critical way Eleanor's future was much different than other women's—she had networks of friends, colleagues, and political supporters, those she had helped and who had helped her around the world and in the smallest towns. She had actively cultivated a rich and diverse network of people. Some served as personal support. Most were a vast resource for her leadership, just as their leadership was nurtured by knowing her. Much of what Eleanor had achieved in the past as a leader, and much of what she was to achieve in her post-White House years depended on these networks.

Eleanor's gift for connecting with people and her strategic use of her connections offer leaders today a model for building, using, and sustaining leadership networks.

Your networks will include some of the people you consider your audience or followers. It will include other leaders as well as people you believe have potential to become followers and leaders. Your networks will include supporters and advisers, friends and mentors, even your family. You need to develop the people connections in your life, understand how other people can enhance your leadership, and look for ways that you can enhance theirs.

Building Networks That Further Your Goals

Each issue you confront presents a different networking situation and offers the opportunity to expand your contacts. When you are facing a leadership challenge, ask yourself: Who can help me achieve my vision, how, and when? In *The Connective Edge*, Jean Lipmen-Blumen talks about leaders skilled in the "social style" who develop "social networks," or "Lego for grownups." These leaders have a strong political sense and they "focus on the connective tissue between people and groups. Their political antennae guide them through the byways of the informal system that operates as a shadow structure inside every formal organization . . . . Some social achievers simply form their own far-flung networks of associates who offer comfort and counsel. Leaders who favor social styles call on relationships without embarrassment, guilt, or discomfort."

What Lipmen-Blumen describes is a two-step process. First you need to be open to the people connections around you, then you need to develop the contacts that promise a mutually helpful relationship. A one-way network is not a network anymore than a one-way conversation is a conversation. The creative energy of your networks lies in discovering the tapestry of information, influence, and support that can be woven between and among your relationships.

As a lobbyist on Capitol Hill I didn't have time to get to know all 535 members of Congress and all the people who worked for them. Yet developing contacts and relationships was the most important part of advocating for or against pieces of legislation; therefore, I had to target the offices of members of Congress that would be most useful for my goals. I also had to build alliances with other lobbyists, working with those who were most closely aligned with my issues. Sometimes I had to extend the network to government agencies and White House personnel or join coalitions with other organizations. Often, I had to enlist the help of thousands of people in my membership-based organization. This meant building a field network of local leaders who were willing to carry the vision forward. Each issue was different, but each required an intentional, targeted strategy for network building.

When I decided to become a writer, I realized I needed a network as well. My writing could only motivate others if it was read, and that meant developing myriad connections in order to get published and get my written work in people's hands. As a lobbyist I had a finite, well-defined group to target, now the universe of potential connections was less defined. All the writers in Washington weren't clustered in offices in one part of town, and it wasn't easy to define what a writer's network would look like. I had to be intentional about asking questions, listening well, and reaching out.

I started my network with the editor who accepted my first opinion piece for the *Washington Post*. After the piece ran, I called and asked if he'd have lunch with me. He did, and we had a casual friendship for eight years that helped me break into the writing world. I also joined the National Writer's Union, which has given me a high-tech network of email connections and support on handling a variety of issues. And I've often discovered that my lobbying background is useful to other writers.

Wherever I met people I looked for writing connections. At the park where I run my dog, I met another writer who was just starting out. How did I find out what she did? I asked her. We've supported each other and shared our writing for several years with great success. Thanks to her advice, I attended a writer's event where I met my agent. At another event this same friend introduced me to a more experienced "ghost" writer who has become a friend. This woman has brought me into her network of poets, editors, and novelists. Writing this book has meant building an extended network of readers, critics, marketing contacts, and boosters. (Just look at the acknowledgments!)

Targeted, intentional networking is part of every leader's job in every sector. A recent article in *Forbes Small Business* discussed "smart events" networking for entrepreneurs. At speed pitching events, organizers hook up high-tech CEOs with investors by giving the money seekers exactly five minutes to make their pitch. Other events provide a relaxed atmosphere, including drinks and games where CEOs meet investors, service providers, and potential hires. Joining trade associations helps these entrepreneurs target their networking by keeping them informed about upcoming events.

Women managers have shown themselves to be particularly effective at intentionally creating the mutually supportive connections that make for effective leadership. According to Body Shop founder and CEO Anita Roddick, "These women build alliances, bring people together, and most importantly they develop intimate, informal networks. Their biggest strength is communication."

Reach Out and Connect

Once you've targeted the connections you need, you have to have an ability and willingness to reach out to people. You need to connect with them in a way that will let you present your vision and enlist their help. If you have found your leadership passion, if you have a clear and compelling vision, you should welcome the chance to share it with others.

Many people find it hard to be outgoing. That's where Eleanor offers inspiration. Painfully shy as a child and even into her early adulthood, she overcame emotional hurdles and learned to reach out to people for the sake of what she believed in.

No one who saw the solemn child called "Granny" by her own mother could have imagined the people person that Eleanor would become. After marrying Franklin, Eleanor admitted that she lost her "self-confidence and ability to look after myself." For ten years she was "always just getting over having a baby or about to have one." Her life became defined by others, especially her overbearing mother-in-law, Sara. Family and society friends circled her life in a knot that she rarely could break.

Eleanor admitted that at first she found few issues compelling enough to drive her into confrontations or unpleasantness, but as her leadership passion grew Eleanor accepted conflict as inevitable "so we can prove our strength and demand respect for our wishes." She saw the need for networking to help women organize for change. "Women must become more conscious of themselves as women and of their ability to function as a group."

With her battle lines drawn Eleanor built personal connections, learning how to get others to help, support, and work with her. She did it by showing genuine enthusiasm and asking to work with people she particularly liked and respected. She "showed up," shuttling from work sessions to meetings to late night gatherings so that she had many opportunities to meet new people and let them get to know her. She joined organizations, particularly the League of Women Voters, where, according to biographer Blanche Wiesen Cook, she "met and worked with every activist political woman in New York." Eleanor actively expanded her circle of contacts, and when the presidential nominating convention of 1924 came around, she had a powerful network to assist her in her first big political battle.

Charles F. Murphy, dignified and soft-spoken, had long been the boss of the rough-sided political organization called Tammany Hall. A practical politician, he hadn't supported women's suffrage, but had told Frances Perkins in 1915 that if women won the vote, "I hope you will remember that you would make a good Democrat."

By 1924 Perkins and many other women social reformers *had* become Democrats, and they were demanding the right to name their own delegates to the national convention. Murphy stood in their way. He insisted that the men leaders would do the choosing, and he didn't expect opposition.

But Boss Murphy hadn't counted on Eleanor. She took on the fight with Murphy, drawing on the network of women activists she had developed since rising to a leadership role in the League of Women Voters in 1921. By 1924 she had moved her office to the women's division of the Democratic State Committee. Her broad circle included the lawyer Elizabeth Read and her partner, the journalist and publicist Esther

Lape. Caroline O'Day, widow to an heir of the Standard Oil fortune, worked with Eleanor alongside Elinor Morgenthau. Eleanor's friends and business partners Nancy Cook and Marion Dickerman helped travel the state to organize women. Frances Perkins, a state labor commissioner in 1924, and labor organizer Rose Schneiderman were also part of Eleanor's political network.

Eleanor believed a woman had "to checkmate as well as her masculine opponent" when playing the game of politics, and in an indication of her sophistication about the power of networks and alliances, she went on, "or it may be that with time she will learn to make an ally of her opponent, which is even better politics." Eleanor firmly believed that "women must learn to play the game as men do."

In the Murphy battle Eleanor went for checkmate first. "I imagine it is just a question of which [Murphy] dislikes most," she wrote Franklin, "giving me my way or having me give the papers a grand chance for a story by telling the whole story at the women's dinner Monday night and by insisting on recognition on the floor of the convention and putting the names in nomination." She had already secured the written endorsement of forty-nine associate Democratic county chairmen.

But Murphy wouldn't budge and Eleanor denounced his stubbornness at the women's dinner, insisting that women would work "with" men, not "for" them. Leading a lobbying committee she headed off to see Governor Al Smith the next day. Smith backed the women. That did it for Murphy, who finally caved in to Eleanor's demands. She told the press, "We go into the campaign feeling that our party has recognized us as an independent part of the organization." Four years later she would work in and mobilize an even broader network in the unsuccessful effort to elect Smith president of the United States.

Eleanor succeeded in the Murphy fight by activating her network—Franklin and Louis Howe, who gave political advice; her friends and colleagues, who gave advice and support; local Democratic organizations, who rallied behind her; and the governor, who lent the weight of his approval. The woman who had been an introverted somber young person had transformed herself into a figure so well respected and well known that many called her "the greatest woman of [her] generation." She had learned that people welcomed her interest and she gained the confidence to expand her networks further. By 1928, she was finance chair for women in the Democratic Party in New York, vice chair of the Women's City Club, chair of the Non-Partisan Legislative Committee, and on the boards of the Foreign Policy Association and the City Housing Corporation.

The only way to build your contacts and networks is to be proactive like Eleanor. In her book, *Play Like a Man, Win Like a Woman*, CNN Executive Vice President Gail Evans tells a revealing story. She had given a talk to a group of young journalists. Twenty eager young women handed her their card hoping to make a contact for their future. "I showed interest in these women's ambitions. I encouraged them to write. I told them if they were really serious about new jobs, they should start strategizing and get in touch with me," Evans writes. But experience had taught her that she would be disappointed. "In fact, I didn't hear from any of them."

The young women Evans describes had come to the right place at the right time with the apparent intention of making new contacts. They had targeted a powerful person for their network. Yet they failed to take the crucial step in making Evans part of their network.

Adding names to your email list doesn't mean you've increased your contacts. You need to get on people's radar screen, or more concretely, on *their* email list as well. This means being intentional about following through even if it takes communicating many times and in different ways with the person you hope to bring into your network. Send an article that you think might interest the person. Invite him or her to an event or out for coffee, or just send an occasional note or email to keep in touch.

Like Eleanor, you need to be proactive in building people-based connections around your leadership goals. Gail Segal Elmore, former managing director for Bank of America, advises, "Just get out there and be confident others want to meet with you." Confidence in your vision combined with action—that's the best way to develop your leadership network.

$\mathscr{B}$e Open and Inclusive

Your networks should be as inclusive as possible. In her book *Why Good Girls Don't Get Ahead . . . But Gutsy Girls Do*, Kate White advises forming alliances with "the gatekeepers to power: secretaries . . . the keepers of information. In every company there are people in middle or low rank who possess critical information . . . people who perform basic services that one day you may need urgently. Like the print shop, the mail room, and computer services."

Eleanor put great weight on deciding whom to include as a friend, but she erred on the side of being inclusive. "The narrower you make the circle of your friends, the narrower will be your experience of people and the narrower will your interests become. It is an important part of one's personal choices to decide to widen the circle of one's acquaintances whenever one can," she wrote. Although the term "networking" wasn't in vogue during Eleanor's time, she was the quintessential networker, sifting her relationships through the same sieve of morality that underpinned her vision. She refused to judge people's value by "prestige, income, or such shallow and vulgar standards." Today inclusiveness and collaboration are seen as leadership strengths and highly identified with women leaders. For Eleanor, however, following her natural style often meant defying conventional standards.

Eleanor's networks included close personal friends, dignitaries, socialites, and professionals of every stripe, but she also included trade unionists and blue collar and service workers, including her own house workers and drivers. She saw everyone within her circle as having "a dignified, necessary contribution to make." And Franklin became more than her friend and husband. He served as Eleanor's political adviser as well as her most powerful contact for political change.

The breadth of Eleanor's networks even reached into her family life. Like many women, Eleanor acted out her leadership in her role as a mother. She tried to instill in her children her vision of an egalitarian world. One of her tactics was to expose them to her wide range of friends. Sailing at Campobello one summer her sons were spellbound by the stories told them by a woman union leader who had come to visit. Later Eleanor listened with delight as her son told a friend that some of "Mummy's strange friends" were visiting. "But they are darned interesting, too," he added.

Eleanor expanded her networks to young people as well. She focused on "the relationship between youth and older people," which she believed needed to be developed for mutual benefit. In an article in 1935 she signaled her interest in building connections between generations, a network that she would more fully develop during the New Deal years. "We older people know that we don't always succeed as easily as these young ones think they can. Yet I doubt if we should smile. I think that we should welcome their help, and find places where this tremendous energy that is in youth—

if it cannot be used immediately in making a living—may at least be used where it is so greatly needed today."

Most dramatically, Eleanor included black Americans among her close friends and contacts. In the highly segregated world of her youth she had rarely met a black person but by the time she entered the White House she was ready to defy segregationists by befriending blacks and including them in her life and work. She formed her first close friendship across racial lines with Mary McLeod Bethune. A contemporary of Eleanor's, Bethune was the daughter of former slaves. She founded a college and became a nationally recognized civil rights leader. Along with other blacks breaking through the color barrier, Bethune often dined at the White House and attended other functions there at Eleanor's invitation.

By her bold insistence on expanding her network in unconventional ways, Eleanor not only gained allies and resources for furthering her vision of social justice, she also changed the nation's perceptions about being open and inclusive. A reporter made this clear to Eleanor at FDR's last inaugural. The first lady's energy began flagging as the night wore on and she had not circulated among the many rooms full of supporters. A woman reporter realized that Eleanor hadn't grasped the import of the guests who swirled around her. "I want to tell you if this were the first inauguration, I would write a story that would be headlined all over the country—NEGROES INVADE WHITE HOUSE. I have just walked through the rooms. There are many colored people here. All have come because of their jobs or invitations. Some are friends of yours, but all are here because they have the right to be, and it is not news any more."

Deborah Schneider, a thirty-year-old lawyer in the midst of a career change, has an attitude like Eleanor's when it comes to networking. "I see everyone as a friend and I try to be completely genuine. I don't separate friends from other people who can help me and who I can help. They're all part of my network."

Before Schneider decided to change her job to become a career counselor and author, she worked in Congress and then for two start-up dot-com companies. "Thanks to my networking I never had to look for a job," she said. "I'm proactive about seeking out people to help me, but it's a give and take relationship where I enjoy helping them too. I didn't know anyone when I moved from D.C. to San Francisco, but after a few month's I had a party for two hundred people." Schneider always made the call to a potential contact, went to the event where she could meet people, and took every opportunity to reach out, "because otherwise, you may miss a great chance to build your network."

Your network is all around you. Are you teaching or taking a course? Active in community groups? Part of a house of worship? A member of a sports team? All of these activities offer the opportunity to expand your network in support of your leadership goals.

Be the Connector

Social leaders, according to Jean Lipmen-Blumen, "do not jealously guard their roster of friends and associates. For them, networks are simply the fastest route to reaching anyone's objectives. They automatically utilize the same methods to help other people in their tasks, as well. They readily introduce people to one another. Once they identify the problem you are tackling, they quickly link you to people with similar interests or the appropriate expertise." This is the way Eleanor worked between and among her friends and contacts.

In describing Eleanor's political work in the 1920s, Blanche Wiesen Cook writes, "Above all, ER understood that information and organization required local clubs and political centers, a network of women active in every town and village connected to one another through meetings, debates, round-table discussions, luncheons, dinner parties, and personal friendships."

During the White House years, Eleanor took every opportunity to link those in her networks to each other. For example, in 1944, when postwar planning moved into high gear, Eleanor worried about full employment for returning soldiers and women workers who would be displaced. She invited the young Walter Reuther, head of the auto workers union, to come to Hyde Park and give her his ideas about postwar industrial needs. Reuther disagreed with a report done by Bernard Baruch who headed up a unit on postwar economic adjustment. Eleanor told Baruch, a former financier and longtime associate, of Reuther's concerns. Then she acted as "mailman" between the two, believing they would educate and help each other through exchanging ideas.

Leaders who are good networkers like to help other people. They are the "connectors" that Malcolm Gladwell talks about in his book, *The Tipping Point*. They know many, many people and they spread new information to their ever-growing roster of contacts, but they also link contacts together. Sometimes they take themselves out of the connected loop. They master what sociologist Mark Granovetter called the "weak tie," a friendly yet casual social connection. According to Gladwell, connectors enhance their ability to lead by cultivating weak ties. "Acquaintances . . . represent a source of social power, and the more acquaintances you have, the more powerful you are," Gladwell writes.

Leaders who are connectors are as quick to assess another person's needs and offer connective advice as they are to seek help for their own projects. To be effective, connecting doesn't have to be confined to business-related issues. I've connected people with other contacts in my networks to help them find jobs or get professional advice, but I've also set up blind dates. I think of myself as a "full-service" networker. I'm glad I can be a resource to other people because of who I know, and I don't hesitate to use who I know to help others reach their goals, and, ultimately, to help me reach my own goals.

Maintain Your Networks and Connections

As your contacts grow and you develop various networks over time, it's important to remember to nurture these relationships. Keep in touch even if it's only occasionally or over a gap of years. Sometimes you'll lose contact with people, but don't let time keep you from reconnecting. Technology has made this a great deal easier. Keep up your email lists, and consider a personal Web site so people can find you and keep up with you.

I found a friend from twenty years ago because she was listed on a Web site for her high school reunion. I remembered she had been interested in filmmaking, and when my daughter also became interested in this field, I decided to try and find my old friend. Sure enough, she had made some independent films and is now a writer in Hollywood. We reconnected and she's helped me with this book, and has given my daughter some career advice.

Of course, Eleanor didn't have the benefit of technology, but she loved to correspond by writing. Her letters to her family and closest friends are voluminous. Whole volumes, such as *Mother & Daughter, The Letters of Anna and Eleanor Roosevelt* or *Empty Without You, The Intimate Letters of Eleanor Roosevelt and Lorena Hickok* are dedicated to these letters. Eleanor found time to write to friends, ordinary citizens, and people throughout her vast network of relationships. She kept this correspondence up until she died.

Eleanor maintained her networks through her affiliations as well. The Democratic Women's Committee had offered Eleanor her first chance to draw political blood in the 1920s. Eleanor stayed an active member throughout her life, celebrating the opening of a New York headquarters in 1956 and leading an all-day workshop on campaign strategy and lobbying. Like Eleanor, you must build your networks, but you must also work to maintain them.

Effective leaders set up a variety of networks, look for alliances, and foster connections to help them achieve their goals. James Kouzes and Barry Posner state this well in *The Leadership Challenge*. "Being connected to people who can open doors, offer support and backing, provide information, mentor and teach, and add to one's reputation increases power," they write. You can increase your own power by forming strategic relationships, and you can strengthen others in the same way. You need to be a connector who advances your own leadership vision by using a sharing community that you create.

In his book *On Leadership*, in the chapter titled "The Knitting Together," John W. Gardner writes, "Leaders must build outside networks of allies in the many other segments of society whose cooperation is required for a significant result. Wise chief executives place in key positions throughout their organizations individuals who are networkers by inclination." You may be a networker by inclination, or you can become a networker by intention. Either way, you will find that your networks will sustain you in many ways and throughout your life, just as Eleanor's did for her.

$\mathcal{E}$LEANOR'S WAY

- Look for opportunities to network wherever you can. Take the initiative in meeting new people and looking for ways that you can help each other.

- Be broad and inclusive in building your network. Sometimes the most helpful contact is the least obvious.

- Recognize the give-and-take of networking. Look for ways you can help people meet their goals and assess how they can help you meet yours.

- Be creative in bringing people into your sphere. Try asking their opinion and show that you listened. Invite them to a social event. Fix them up for a date. Look for ways to show that you care.

- Look for areas of mutual interest, seek out others with shared goals, then form alliances that seek to meet everyone's needs.

- Understand that networks and alliances are built over time. Be intentional about developing the right networks and alliances for your goals, and be patient.

- People who seem peripheral to your goals now may be central to them in the future. Be open to everyone.

- Be a "connector" linking people in your networks to each other.

- Don't overlook the social side of networking. Some people in your networks will become friends. Some friends will become part of a business network.

- Lead by fully using all the resources your networks provide.

CHAPTER ELEVEN

Embrace Risk

"What matters now, as always,
is not what we can't do:
it is what we can and must do."
—*ER*

They strode into the white granite grandeur of Union Station in Washington, D.C., on December 30, 1945 headed for a specially commissioned train en route to New York City, where the massive liner *Queen Elizabeth* waited. The gray ship that had ferried troops in the war would carry the United States delegates to London for the first meeting of the United Nations.

The delegates' entourage included advisers and assistants, more than one hundred of them in all. A motorcade of army limousines waited at Pennsylvania Station to take this eminent group of men to the pier—U.S. Secretary of State James Byrnes, Assistant Secretary of State Edward Stettinius, and Senators Tom Connally and Arthur Vandenberg. When they reached the dock, reporters swarmed forward for statements, cameras flashed, and the group followed escorts to staterooms to prepare for the ocean voyage.

Hours after the motorcade's sirens and lights faded, the fifth official member of the U.S. delegation drove up in her own car. Dressed in black, Eleanor arrived late and alone in a rainy chill that seemed to reflect her spirits. She didn't know she could bring a secretary, so Malvina (Tommy) Thompson had stayed behind, dealing with the hundreds of letters that still poured in daily. Eleanor felt "heavyhearted at the thought of crossing the Atlantic Ocean alone in January," but she was also determined to take on this new challenge. She climbed the gangplank terrified to take a job she knew nothing about. The grief that had been her shadow since Franklin's death still followed her.

President Truman had called only a few weeks before, as Eleanor was having lunch with Franklin Jr. in her Washington Square apartment. "Oh, no! It would be impossible!" her son heard her exclaim. "How could I be a delegate to help organize the United Nations when I have no background or experience in international meetings?" His voice firm and full of the flat vowels of Missouri's heartland, Truman pressed her to agree. He needed Eleanor to carry forward her husband's legacy by reminding the other delegates at the assembly of FDR's vision. Truman also wanted to keep Eleanor on his political team as a link to black voters and the new president had genuine admiration for the woman he still called "First Lady."

With encouragement from her children and close friends, Eleanor reluctantly agreed to serve. The press didn't share her uncertainty. "She has convictions and doesn't hesitate to fight for them," wrote newspaper columnist Thomas Stokes. He saw her as the best person to "represent the little people of this country, indeed the world."

Eleanor wasn't so sure. She had no expertise in international affairs; she didn't even know parliamentary procedure.

She felt the weight of being the first woman, sure that her performance would determine whether or not women would be welcomed and valued in the future. She underestimated the leadership and moral authority she would bring to London, writing that she would take her "sincere desire to understand the problems of the rest of the world and our relationship to them; a real good will for all peoples throughout the world; a hope that I shall be able to build a sense of personal trust and friendship with my co-workers." Desire, goodwill, and hope? Humble sentiments from a leader who also brought a sharp intellect, energy, focus, determination, courage, and conviction. Although she didn't realize it, Eleanor had started down the road to becoming "First Lady of the World."

In her stateroom that first night, Eleanor found a pile of blue papers, mostly marked "secret." She immediately got to work on the dull and difficult State Department documents so boring they nearly put her to sleep. She struggled with her sense of inadequacy, worried that she couldn't understand plain English. She compensated by working hard. Rising early, she had breakfast at the captain's table then attended every briefing, read, and read more, and developed her relationships with the other delegates. Briskly walking the deck in rain, fog, or sunshine, she used the time to talk with other delegates and advisers.

One day Senator Vandenberg came up to Eleanor in the passageway to her cabin. In his deep voice he said, "We would like to know if you would serve on Committee Three?" Eleanor was baffled. What was Committee Three? What group had selected her? Were the men meeting behind her back? After all, she didn't even know who had been placing documents for her to read in her stateroom. But she agreed to take the assignment asking simply, "Will you or someone kindly see that I get as much information as possible on Committee Three?"

Eleanor quickly discovered that Committee Three dealt with humanitarian, educational, and cultural questions. She suspected that the men had conspired to put her in a backwater, and would have been certain had she known how hard some of the other delegates had worked to convince Truman not to nominate her. As it was, she could just imagine them saying, "Oh, no! We can't put Mrs. Roosevelt on the political committee. What would she do on the budget committee? Does she know anything about legal questions? Ah, here's the safe spot for her—Committee Three. She can't do much harm there!" But as she read through the committee papers she sensed that her pigeonhole "might be much more important than had been expected."

When she reached London, Eleanor found her room at Claridge's Hotel overflowing with flowers and invitations from dignitaries and old friends. She quickly set a routine. Her day started with personal work before she headed off to committee meetings, then she crammed her evenings with dinners, cocktail parties, and endless speeches. Outwardly, Eleanor appeared lively and gracious; inwardly, however, she carried the weight of the risk she had taken plunging into a new life. "I knew that as the only woman on the delegation I was not very welcome." Then her opportunity to prove her leadership skills arrived.

More than a million refugees living in displaced persons camps in Western Europe were unwilling, based on fear of imprisonment or worse, to return to their countries. The Communists declared that any refugees who didn't want to return home, and most were from the East, were traitors who should be forced to return. Western countries disagreed. Suddenly the delegates on Committee Three were hotly debating the most contentious issue of East-West relations.

Debate in the committee was endless. "I have spent nine hours of meetings these last two days," Eleanor wrote, "to try to frame a resolution on refugees to which the Russians and ourselves can agree." A week later she wrote, "Committee meeting was one long wrangle." Eleanor called for a vote; the Russians pushed for delay. Negotiations inched forward, but finally it came down to three points of disagreement with the Russians. Eleanor spoke briefly and clearly in opposition. When the vote was taken, the Russians lost decisively. But they weren't finished.

Andrei Vishinsky, a former prosecutor in the Soviet Union known as a shrewd debater and strategist, challenged the committee and demanded to speak to the delegates in plenary session. The United States would have to respond. The men of the American delegation huddled anxiously. The only delegate who knew the issue was the woman they had placed on Committee Three. Hesitantly, they asked Eleanor to take the floor and say a "few words."

Vishinsky had spoken with emotional power calling tolerance for the refugees a dangerous weakness. When he finished, Eleanor strode to the podium in a tailored black dress and black hat. She countered Vishinsky by pleading for tolerance and shrewdly invoking the history of freedom fighters like Simon Bolivar of Latin America. After more than six hours of debate the Russians were again defeated. At one A.M., Eleanor crowned her leadership of the delegation by extending a personal olive branch to her adversaries. "I shook hands and said I admired their fighting qualities and I hoped some day on that kind of question we would be on the same side."

Eleanor, moving into her first role of formal authority since her brief tenure with the Office of Civilian Defense, had proved her leadership ability to her skeptical colleagues. The hostility of the other American delegates began to fade. When John Foster Dulles, an alternate, said good-bye to her he added, "I feel I must tell you that when you were appointed I thought it terrible and now I think your work here has been fine!" Back in Washington, Senator Vandenberg quipped, "I take back everything I ever said about her, and believe me it's been plenty."

Eleanor risked taking the U.N. appointment despite her fears of personal failure. By doing so she gained the chance to forge a new life and new identity free of the constraints of the White House. Within a few years, her work with the U.N. would lead to her crowning achievement: passage of the Universal Declaration of Human Rights.

Eleanor's work at the U.N. is a model of turning risk into reward, something every leader must embrace. In a chapter titled, "The Importance of Taking Risks," James Kouzes and Barry Posner write in their book *The Leadership Challenge* that experimentation and innovation to improve things necessarily put leaders and those who work with them at risk. "One of the most glaring differences between the leader and the bureaucrat," they write, "is the leader's inclination to encourage risk taking, to encourage others to step out into the unknown rather than play it safe."

Risk Takers Believe in Themselves

Women have a particular need to be risk takers because male-dominated corporate hierarchies still maintain artificial barriers for women's promotion. These barriers include denying women job-connected chances to take risks. A study in 2001 by the recruiting firm Korn/Ferry International showed that in the United States, women executives are leaving jobs to start their own businesses because they are looking for the opportunity to take risks, to have a seat at the decision-making table, and to increase their pay.

In *Women on Power*, Sue J. M. Freeman writes, "Women who want increasing autonomy and responsibility at work are not staying at their jobs in an endless wait for promotion. Many have done all within their power to climb a corporate ladder where the top steps were missing. When the limits became clear to them and they still felt the need for further advancement, they took initiative and sought other prospects." Sometimes this means changing jobs. Increasingly, it means becoming entrepreneurs.

Even in situations where women have a fair chance for advancement, taking risks is still a valued leadership trait. In her landmark book on corporate power dynamics, *Men and Women of the Corporation,* Rosabeth Moss Kanter discusses activities as a route to power. Activities have to be extraordinary, visible, and relevant to organizational problems in order to enhance a person's power in the company. "The rewards go to innovators, not to the second ones to do something," Kantor writes in explaining how leadership is perceived. But innovation is risky at the same time that it can be "power-enhancing." Corporate risk takers who succeeded had demonstrated that they could take on tough assignments and "developed charisma in the eyes of the less daring," according to Kanter.

Susan P. Garson, vice president of Wilmington Savings Fund Society, takes risks on a regular basis as part of her work as a commercial relationship manager. "Early in my professional career, one of my mentors challenged me to overcome my insecurities, which were preventing me from taking risks in my job," Garson explains. "She encouraged me to believe in myself, which gave me greater confidence in how I handle my clients' accounts."

A recent loan request from an architectural design and construction firm illustrates Garson's role as a risk taker. A builder of multimillion dollar homes, the firm wanted to expand by going into the manufacture of the millwork they installed in the homes they built. Garson had to decide if the company could expand successfully. She looked at their track record and assessed their potential. Unfortunately, the company's financial history didn't strongly support the loan, but Garson had worked closely with them and believed they would make the expanded business work. She convinced a skeptical loan approval committee and got her clients the money. "My reputation was definitely on the line. I am measured by my ability to correctly assess the business's ability to be successful and repay the debt. The first risk is my reputation, but my career growth and ultimately my salary is also on the line." Garson's judgment about the company proved to be right, and she keeps in close touch with them to be sure they continue to meet expectations.

To many women, risk is equated with fear, danger, and other negative consequences. Women are taught to avoid risks from a young age. Studies of teachers have shown the tendency to show girls how to do a task, but to allow boys to try it for themselves. As Gail Evans writes in *Play Like a Man, Win Like a Woman*, "How do you break the training of a lifetime? From the get go men are encouraged to take chances. We are told not to. Little boys are told to get out there and fight. We are told not to. He's 4'2" and he's happy to be guarding a boy who's 5'8". He learns what risk is."

Men also learn to believe in their ability, giving them a platform for risk taking. Studies show that men attribute success to ability, and failure to someone or something outside themselves. This helps them avoid the fear of failing.

Women attribute success to their hard work rather than

ability, and take failure personally. While these tendencies for negative attribution have no basis in the reality of women's competence versus that of men, they do help explain why women avoid risk. After all, who wants to be vulnerable to feelings of failure and blame?

Knowing that you may have a tendency to downplay the credit you deserve can help you to accept risk. Start by believing in your ability as the basis for your success. Of course you worked hard, but don't shy away from believing that you're also smart and especially good at certain things.

Do your own ability assessment. Are you good at building relationships and collaborating with colleagues, being the leader who encourages others to lead? Are you the one who often comes up with the "outside the box" idea that inspires innovation? Are you good at persuading people by listening and reflecting back their interest rather than focusing on their position? Are you strong in math and logic? Are you a good problem solver? Think about your talents and give yourself credit—lots of credit—for them.

When the Risk Is High, Seek Allies

Your support network can help you with taking leadership-related risks. Eleanor had grave doubts about the U.N. appointment, but her network of friends and family were able to help her think through the risks and opportunities. She had to work on changing her appraisal of herself. Compared to the foreign policy experts, the secretary of state and the legions of advisers who were part of the delegation, Eleanor felt highly inadequate. No doubt her friends reminded her that she had taken on equally daunting assignments before. Surely her friends and allies helped her assess her strengths for taking on this new job: her ability to learn quickly, to build powerful relationships, and to seize opportunities to lead.

Talking to others helps clarify our internal arguments, debunking some and deconstructing others. Sometimes we just need cheerleaders, the kind of support that gives us enough "wind beneath our wings" to leap forward.

This was true for Stephanie Jones when, in 1994, she got a call from the Clinton administration asking her to take a presidential appointment in the Department of Education in the Chicago regional office. Jones, thirty-four and single, was teaching at the Chase College of Law in Kentucky, on her way to a tenure-track position. She felt secure and comfortable. Even though she had worked in the Clinton presidential campaign, she had never considered, or particularly wanted, a government job. "This was a complete change of career direction," Jones explained, "I didn't really know what it would be about."

The Clinton offer meant moving to a new city and taking over a high-level office without much experience to back her up. What if she didn't fit into that kind of bureaucracy? Why take the risk? she asked herself. Then she talked to the most important person in her support network—her father, Nathaniel. He gave her the reality check she needed by talking about his own experience with risk.

In 1969, Nathaniel Jones had faced a similar dilemma when Roy Wilkins offered him the job of general counsel for the NAACP. "I'm going to give you the same advice a friend gave me," Jones, now a circuit court judge, told his daughter. "You don't have a choice. When the president of the United States asks you to serve you have to do it, just like I had to serve when I was asked. The rest will take care of itself." Judge Jones's advice resounded with leadership values that his daughter had incorporated from childhood. "I immediately knew he was right," she said.

Stephanie Jones moved to Chicago at the worst possible time, a bleak and frigid January that left her asking herself, "What did I do?" But as the chief spokesperson for the secretary of education in a six-state region, Jones soon found her footing. Her role as the senior staff person in an office of 250 people offered challenges and opportunities that gave her a new, powerful career direction. Today, Jones is chief of staff to a member of Congress.

Whether you turn to family, friends, or others you feel could offer help, find the support system that will help you take a chance and grow as a leader.

Risk Takers Are Failures Who Succeeded

If you take risks, you will fail. No one succeeds all the time. But failing doesn't make you a failure. You have to remember that every risk taker has failed and will fail again. Just think of risk takers as "failures who succeeded." If you are persistent in taking on challenges that stretch your leadership, you will succeed. Even your failures hold the seeds of success, since successful risk takers learn from every experience, analyzing what went wrong and how to do better the next time.

Eleanor had a grand string of failures to her credit, from the Arthurdale planned community to calls for social reform that never became law. But within each failure lay the building blocks of success. Arthurdale never became a utopia of economic independence in Depression-ravaged West Virginia. But its existence challenged naysayers to find a better solution, gave hope to some desperate families, and taught Eleanor about real-world economics and government experimentation.

Sports also present a clear view of the power of failure. From Mia Hamm on the soccer field to Chamique Holdsclaw on the basketball court to the women softball players at the park down the street, every athlete learns more from taking risks and failing than from an easy success. One of Eleanor's happiest memories was from her teenage years, when she was chosen for the field hockey team at Allenswood, her boarding school in England. She loved competition. But competition by its nature encompasses defeat as well as victory. In playing field competition, everyone risks losing every time he or she plays. Every top athlete talks about the mental toughness it takes to face the risk of losing. And every one of them will acknowledge the role failure plays in learning to be mentally tough.

Resist the urge to wallow in personal blame over failure. Don't engage in a mental assault on yourself. If things don't work out the way they were supposed to, assess the damage, look for solutions, and move on.

Women have had less opportunity than men to experience risk, to learn that failure is rarely as dire in retrospect as it is when we worry about it ahead of time. The worry continues to lead us to choose safety over comfort, stifling our leadership in prisons of concern. This is a particularly self-defeating cycle, because the only way to become a risk taker is to take risks, fail sometimes, succeed sometimes, and keep learning from the experience.

Being willing to challenge your fear of failure, take on risks and successfully negotiate your way to success is key to powerful leadership. "Obviously it requires effort to use your potentialities to the best of your ability," Eleanor wrote, "to stretch your horizon, to grasp every opportunity as it comes, but it is certainly more interesting than holding off timidly, afraid to take a chance, afraid to fail."

*O*ptimism Is Power

One important characteristic of leaders who successfully confront their fear of failure, who take risks and inspire others to do the same, is optimism. But you can't just tell yourself to be sunny about every event, and optimism doesn't mean being a nonstop cheerleader or living in a fantasy world. Optimism that is powerful enough to overcome internal fears has the muscle of experience, culture, and faith behind it. It is both a mental discipline and a worldview.

Eleanor put it best in response to a question about why she wasn't more of a cynic. She explained that she chose "affirmation" over "negation." "It is true that I am fundamentally an optimist, that I am congenitally hopeful. I do not believe that good always conquers evil, because I have lived a long time in the world and seen that it is not true. I do not seek the pot of gold at the foot of the rainbow or think that 'everything will have a happy ending' because I would like it to. It is not wishful thinking that makes me a hopeful woman. Over and over, I have seen, under the most improbable circumstances, that man can remake himself, that he can even remake his world if he cares enough to try."

Many people find it hard to be optimistic. They take a "glass half empty" view of the world. They come to believe that their pessimism is logical, that their experience has taught them to be negative, that they are protecting themselves from disappointment by expecting the worst. They get stuck in self-reinforcing loops of blame-guilt-pessimism. But no one can lead from a negative perspective because pessimism has no motivational power. Why would anyone follow someone who acts and talks like success is impossible?

Leaders motivate those they want to enlist in their vision by communicating, even radiating, a sense of the possible. They lift the hearts and dreams of others through ideas infused with hope. They convince others that collective work will reap wonderful rewards, despite—or even because of—the obstacles along the way.

Author John W. Gardner calls this "tough-minded optimism." He writes, "Leaders must instill in their people a hard-bitten morale that mixes our natural American optimism with a measure of realism. To sustain hope one need not blind oneself to reality. People need to know the worst—about the evils to be remedied, the injustices to be dealt with, the catastrophes to be averted."

Eleanor's optimism rooted itself in faith. She often drew inspiration from prayer and religious affirmations, regularly carrying a prayer in her purse. Shortly after becoming first lady, Eleanor wrote that some kind of faith, "a firm conviction that there is a reason and a meaning" behind hardship, gave people the courage and strength to take positive action. Her faith carried her through a lifetime. When she served at the U.N., Eleanor would kneel by her bedside each night and repeat the same prayer. She asked God to "deliver us from fretfulness and self-pitying; make us sure of the good we cannot see and of the hidden good in the world. Open our eyes to simple beauty all around us and our hearts to the loveliness men hide from us because we do not try to understand them. Save us from ourselves and show us a vision of a world made new." Through this prayer, Eleanor renewed and reinforced her optimistic view of the world.

Religious faith is not a prerequisite for optimism, but faith is—faith that you can reach your goals, faith that you can lead others toward a transforming vision, faith that dark moments pass into moments of light and clarity. If you don't draw this faith from religion, you can draw it from experience and habits of the mind and heart.

Start developing a more optimistic disposition with three attitude adjustment strategies. First, choose as a model someone who exemplifies the kind of positive attitude you hope to develop. Either pick someone you know or someone, such as Eleanor, whom you admire and have read about. When you catch yourself being negative, think of what that person would do and try to do the same.

Second, just as you took the "shoulds" out of your vocabulary, take out the "I can'ts." Don't let yourself off the hook. Don't passively accept your own expectations and beliefs. Question your negative assumptions. Remind yourself of your successes. Draw strength from positive experiences and use them to be your own best booster. Then try saying "I can," whether you believe it or not. Fight the urge to reject your own words. Spin out an "I can" story about what you hope to accomplish, either in your head or, more powerfully, in writing.

The third strategy is practicing acceptance. When something negative happens that you can't control, rather than getting angry or frustrated, say, "This is my opportunity to practice acceptance." You can start with small things, such as the person who cut you off on the highway and sped away. What do you accomplish by fuming for the next several miles or hours? Use the affront as a small chance to practice acceptance. Say to yourself, "Great, another chance to practice acceptance," and turn it into a habit of mind. You can never control everything or everyone, and when you try, you add to your anxiety and pessimism. This ability to practice acceptance is a recognized characteristic of leaders.

The psychologist Abraham Maslow studied people he termed "self-actualized," those who made full use of their talents and potential. These personalities, and he included Eleanor in the group, accepted themselves and "the frailties and sins, weaknesses, and evils of human nature in the same unquestioning spirit with which one accepts the characteristics of nature." According to Maslow, self-actualized people accept human nature without being resigned to it.

One dramatic instance where Eleanor demonstrated her capacity for acceptance came after Franklin's death, as she began packing up the house at Hyde Park. Little time had passed since the shock of learning that Lucy Mercer Rutherford had been at Franklin's side when he died. Even more devastating, Eleanor had discovered that her daughter had helped arrange liaisons between the two. Now, as she sorted through Franklin's belongings, Eleanor found a small watercolor portrait of her husband painted by Madame Shoumatoff, the same artist who at Lucy Mercer Rutherford's invitation had been painting Franklin on the day he died.

Franklin was gone. The past could not be changed. Eleanor handed the small portrait to Franklin's cousin, Margaret Suckley, and asked her to send it on to Lucy Mercer Rutherford.

Eleanor's capacity for acceptance allowed her to focus on making positive change, on maintaining a positive view of society and human nature. Like her, you need to accept what you truly can't change or control and move ahead with optimism.

$\mathcal{R}$isk Is a Call to Action

After her triumph at the first U.N. session, Eleanor received another request for her service. The U.N. Charter included a Commission on Human Rights, and Eleanor was asked by the Economic and Social Council of the U.N. to serve on a committee of nine chosen to decide what the commission should do. Buoyed by her work in London, Eleanor readily agreed.

At the first meeting, Eleanor was elected chairwoman. Within weeks, she led the group in recommending that the commission's first task be to write a bill of human rights. "Many of us thought that lack of standards for human rights the world over was one of the greatest causes of friction among the nations," Eleanor wrote, "and that recognition of human rights might become one of the cornerstones on which peace could eventually be based."

Eleanor wielded the gavel over eighteen delegates from countries with widely varied traditions, values, social, and governmental structures. Their task had the potential sweep and moral authority of the Declaration of Independence, but bringing about consensus often boiled down to settling a brawl. For two-and-a-half years, Eleanor wrestled with the Soviets and butted heads with those in love with legalese. Throughout the deliberations, she didn't let the commission members rest. She walked into meetings and called matters to order precisely on time; she scheduled extra sessions and drove the delegates unmercifully. She led by example, working harder and longer than anyone else.

Eleanor took the lead on a project ripe for endless talking and elusive results. The chances of failure were much greater than those of success. A person less committed to action might never have led the group to consensus, might never have gotten to the final goal. But in the fall of 1947 Eleanor pressed her colleagues to finish the draft. She kept evening meetings running well past midnight, and the commission finished in time for the members to go home for Christmas.

The U.N. General Assembly adopted the Universal Declaration of Human Rights the following year without a single country dissenting. Its moral weight has transformed the globe with many newly independent countries adopting it as part of their constitutions in the 1950s and 1960s. After its adoption, Helen Keller wrote to Eleanor saying, "My soul stood erect." The declaration was called "the Magna Carta of mankind" by U.N. Secretary General U Thant.

Like Eleanor, you will find that taking risks demands active leadership. You need to show others what you expect and not just tell them. Do you expect everyone to pitch in on tough assignments? Maximize customer contact? Look for ways to collaborate across teams? Then model that behavior yourself. Make sure you've emphasized the vision that everyone will have a part in achieving the outcome, that everyone is an actor in the collective play. In her essay "Women at the Top," Sue J. M. Freeman describes leaders who take a risky but more rewarding strategy toward others. According to Freeman, these leaders provide the opportunity for their constituency to succeed rather than dictating what to do. A leader "has the courage to move forward, guiding but not dictating, providing just the right balance of support and leeway," Freeman writes.

Eleanor had always led by example and always called on others to do the same. In 1928, after spending nearly a decade as an active political organizer of women in New York State, she wrote a blistering column about women's role in politics. *Redbook* magazine carried the piece, titled "Women Must Learn to Play the Game as Men Do." In it, Eleanor harshly criticized the male party structure that excluded women or only used them for menial tasks.

Although men received the harshest criticism, Eleanor didn't let women off the hook when it came to taking action. She called on women to risk criticism and attacks in order to organize, saying, "If women believe they have a right and duty in political life today, they must learn to talk the language of men. They must not only master the phraseology, but also understand the machinery which men have built through years of practical experience. Against the men bosses there must be women bosses who can talk as equals, with the backing of a coherent organization of women voters behind them."

Thirty years after writing that article, Eleanor still preached the same message, but her audience had grown to encompass the world. In 1958, she wrote about the everyday meaning of universal human rights to individuals. She believed that people looked for equal justice, dignity, and opportunity close to home—in neighborhoods, schools, factories, and offices. But enjoying human rights everywhere, every day, would take action by everyone. "Without concerned citizen action to uphold [rights] close to home," Eleanor wrote, "we shall look in vain for progress in the larger world."

In discussing political leadership, James MacGregor Burns explains that leaders and followers "exchange roles over time and in different political settings." He acknowledges the reality of people being "leaders and followers at the same time." However, as situations and roles shift, leaders have the responsibility of making things happen, Burn notes.

They have "a special role as activators, initiators, mobilizers." They have a special role as risk takers who encourage others to share in bold action. Real, lasting change is the reward for leaders willing to act, willing to lead by example, willing to take risks.

$\mathcal{E}$LEANOR'S WAY

- Leaders are risk takers who seek out and accept new challenges. Be a risk taker.

- Recognize that all risk takers struggle with and overcome internal doubts and fears.

- Focus on your abilities, your talents, your strengths.

- Work hard to overcome risk aversion, particularly in situations where you are in the minority.

- Let other people help and advise you as you prepare to take a chance.

- Accept that you will never be able to plan for or control every contingency; such is the nature of risk.

- Be optimistic. Ask yourself: "What is the worst that can happen?" Get a realistic handle on your doubts and fears, then move ahead. Replace the "I can't" refrain in your mind with "I can."

- Practice the positive—in your mind, in your discussions, in your relationships, in your actions. The glass is always half full if you want it to be.

- Accept that there are problems you can't control and focus on what you can do.

- Lead by example.

- Understand that thinking and talking must lead to action—from yourself and others whom you inspire to act.

- Remember that real change is the reward for leaders who accept risk and take action to bring about their dreams.

CHAPTER TWELVE

Never Stop Learning

"Today, living and learning must go hand in hand."

—ER

*I*n March 1952, the dome of the ornate and majestic Taj Mahal hotel in Bombay gleamed like a beacon. The pride of Indians, after five years of independence could be seen in the faces of a thousand Hindus who stood in front of the hotel, restrained by a police rope line. They sweated as they waited Bombay's heavy dusk. Crowding toward an open car, they were eagerly anticipating "the American Widow Roosevelt." Shouts and applause broke out as she walked from the hotel.

Eleanor stepped into the car but stayed standing, facing the crowd. She bowed her head and pressed her hands together in front of her chest in the traditional Hindu greeting of *namaste* or "reverent salutations." The crowd went wild. They trampled the graceful hotel lawn and toppled pots of flowers as they pressed to get closer to the First Lady of the World. "Eleanor Roosevelt *Zindabad*! Long live Eleanor Roosevelt!" they shouted in the chanting rhythms of the East. Like a conquering hero returning home, Eleanor couldn't satisfy the crowd's enthusiasm. She raised her arms again and again—*namaste, namaste*—she bowed, until suddenly she wavered and nearly collapsed. Stopped by emotion or exhaustion, Eleanor sat down with the help of an aide. She listened to the chants fade as her driver drove off into the night.

The scene made the lead in an extensive *Time* magazine story about "Mrs. R" in April 1952, when, for the third time, Eleanor made the cover. Looking serious and in charge, the drawing portrayed the former first lady in front of a clock with large Roman numerals. The time was a few minutes after nine, suggesting the start of another full day in Eleanor's very full life. At sixty-seven years old, she finished three months of hard work at the U.N. in Paris before undertaking her whirlwind tour of Asia and the Middle East. Her rapport with the Indian people "was an amazing display, not only of the Eleanorean character and its impact upon the feverishly nationalistic (and often anti-American) East, but of Eleanorean durability," *Time* proclaimed.

India's prime minister, Jawaharlal Nehru, had invited Eleanor to visit when he came to America in 1949, but her work with the U.N. had kept her too busy. Her responsibilities at the U.N. had given Eleanor a unique status among the citizens of emerging democracies, who saw her as a friend of humanity.

However, Eleanor realized that she was one of the few Westerners who was viewed kindly. In the Near East, India, and many of the Asiatic countries, "people have a profound distrust of white people," she wrote in a report to President Truman. She understood their feelings as the by-product of years of colonial rule and exploitation by American and European business interests. She worried over their antagonism, and felt that they were being driven into the arms of the Soviets, whose racial and economic ideas were appealing. One Indian diplomat told Eleanor that Americans were willing to save the children of Europe but didn't care "whether the children of India died or lived."

Eleanor suggested to President Truman that he send a "roving ambassador" to the Near East and Asia "to talk philosophy and get a line on attitudes and reasons for those attitudes that we really do not understand . . . ." She offered some names of people she considered suited to the job. Truman's response was, "Why don't you go?" Eleanor had spent the past six years "bustling back and forth across the Atlantic Ocean rather like a harassed commuter," but when the U.N. session ended, she decided to take up Truman's suggestion. "Instead of going back to New York as usual," she told her secretary, "why not go home the long way—around the world."

For Eleanor, the trip was all about learning. But even members of the president's cabinet failed to recognize the power of a lack of presumption and the ability to listen. "Your present trip," wrote Secretary of State Dean Acheson in a note to Eleanor, "will be a means of bringing the American views effectively to some of the Far Eastern peoples." Eleanor knew that the greater task lay in understanding the views that others held. She would do her share of educating about the United States, but she would do more than her share of learning.

Eleanor traveled to Lebanon and Syria. She saw that Israel's triumphant battle for independence in 1948 had left hostility etched on every Arab face. Why, the Syrian press asked Eleanor with bitterness, do you support the Israeli cause? She tried to be even-handed. The United States accepted the idea of a Jewish homeland after World War I, Eleanor patiently explained. "I feel that it practically committed our government to assist in the creation of a government . . . because there cannot be a homeland without a government."

Eleanor visited the Palestinian refugee camps in Jordan and "found them distressing beyond words." Then she went through the Mandelbaum Gate into Israel and learned about the Israeli's massive health program and agricultural renewal policies that had the desert in bloom.

From Israel Eleanor flew to Karachi, Pakistan, as the guest of the All Pakistan Women's Association. Ten thousand people greeted her at the airport. Leading a parade of colorfully decorated camel-drawn carts, she wound her way through the streets of the capital city.

In 1947, Pakistan had been partitioned from India as a predominantly Muslim state. Eleanor could see the difficulties of this split. "The sword of partition," she wrote, "not only divided the land, cutting off crops from markets and factories from raw materials, it also split up everything from debts and revenues to rolling stock and typewriters, including, of course, the army." Then as now, India and Pakistan were in a dangerous stand-off. The two armies "face each other across a line in Kashmir," Eleanor wrote. She learned how defense spending had drained "huge sums badly needed for health, housing, education." She came to understand how the partition lines left millions of Hindus and Sikhs in Muslim territory, and millions of Muslims in India. These facts were what the American people needed to understand about Pakistan and India. It was the only way that America could give "intelligent and effective help," Eleanor concluded.

On landing in New Delhi, Eleanor announced, "I have come here to learn." She set off to address the Parliament. Purse in hand, without notes, she moved from behind the lectern to get closer to the audience. Rather than trumpet American superiority, she searched for common ground. She spoke of mistakes America had made as it developed its democracy then praised the delegates for meeting their problems "in the way our people met theirs."

Eleanor's agenda was packed. She met privately with Nehru and publicly with a group of student dissidents in a jammed hall. She toured rural development projects and placed a wreath where Gandhi had been cremated. As he had done, she sat cross-legged a few inches off the ground at the Harijan colony and tried her hand at an ancient spinning wheel. Crawling on her knees she entered native mud huts. As she reported in her "My Day" column on March 1, 1952, she went to a well-attended women's dinner one night in Lahore, where she taught the Virginia reel to a group of young women using Pakistani music as their accompaniment. After her death, Nehru wrote of Eleanor, "No woman of this generation and few in the annals of history have so well understood and articulated the yearnings of men and women for social justice."

On the way home, Eleanor stopped in Djakarta, Indonesia. Then it was on to Rangoon, Burma, and Manila in the Philippines before returning to Washington. She gave her report to President Truman. Secretary of State Dean Acheson praised what Eleanor had done to "increase understanding of the United States foreign policy objectives." Eleanor, however, took a different view of the trip. She had learned more than she had taught, and she had developed a strong point of view that she argued vigorously: Economic, not military, aid was needed to ensure that India and Pakistan establish stable governments.

Through her travels Eleanor had reached out, as she wrote in *You Learn by Living*, "eagerly and without fear for newer and richer experience." Living and learning, she counseled, required curiosity and "an unquenchable spirit of adventure."

Eleanor's advice goes to the heart of what leaders must do: Look for experience and learn from experience.

Eleanor's passion for individual learning foreshadowed the corporate philosophy of the "learning organization" first discussed by Peter Senge in 1990, in his landmark book, *The Fifth Discipline*. Senge would no doubt say that Eleanor had high levels of "personal mastery," his term for people who are "continually expanding their ability to create the results in life they truly seek. From their quest for continual learning comes the spirit of the learning organization."

Special talents, a big title, and world travel are not required to learn from living or to acquire personal mastery. All you need is an eagerness to probe, investigate, and question. You must be open and attentive to the new information you gain. You must work to move from "status quo" thinking to "new status" thinking.

What Can You Learn Today?

Becoming a leader who is always learning means opening yourself to the possibilities of new ideas and experiences. Sometimes this means seeking them out, but it also means seeing the potential for learning even in situations you didn't expect to be in.

This was true for Naval Commander Yvette C. Brown Wahler. On September 11, 2000, Brown Wahler had her picture taken shaking hands with a young woman who had won the Yahoo! Fantasy Careers Contest. As the defense department's assistant director for recruiting plans, Brown Wahler had the pleasure of seeing more than three thousand young people apply online for the chance to work alongside the Coast Guard, fly on a fighter jet, or parachute with the Golden Knights. Working on new ways to bring young recruits into the armed services was her mission, and the Internet experiment became a grand success.

One year later, on September 11, 2001, Brown Wahler's world changed radically. When 124 Pentagon families were stricken with grief and uncertainty by the devastating terrorist attack on the Pentagon, Brown Wahler suddenly found herself in a new, untried role as head of the hastily established Family Emergency Center. After the first few months, the thirty-nine-year-old mother, five feet tall and full of resolve, won the highest compliments from the families. For Brown Wahler, it was a learning experience. "I won't forget the lessons of the family center," she told the *New York Times*, as she prepared to become one of the few women in naval history to be given command of a warship, the guided missile destroyer *Chafee*. "I'll remember every day why I'm doing what I'm doing. I'll see both sides. I'll see my crew before me, and I'll see their families, too, and the war and sorrow that can come." Brown Wahler also used her Emergency Center experience to develop a preparedness plan for use at the Pentagon.

Brown Wahler's unexpected assignment led her to new insights, a broader perspective and a new depth of understanding of her mission as a naval officer. Her attitude of analyzing and learning from her experience exemplifies what learning leaders do. They see every new experience as a learning laboratory. They rise to new challenges at the same time as they seek deeper understanding of the learning that is going on. Sometimes it takes time to realize what you can take away from a new experience. That's why it's important to stay highly attuned to potential learning opportunities. You may have to store something you learned. Eventually, however, it will prove valuable at another time and in another context.

Eleanor had strong feelings about being open to learning opportunities. "You must be interested in anything that comes your way," she advised. She might have added that you must be interested in *anyone* as well. An insurance salesman in New York recalled being stuck in an elevator with Eleanor for ten minutes. "I think that I am the most uninteresting fellow in the world," he recalled, "and yet Mrs. Roosevelt wanted to know everything about me, as if I were equal to her." No doubt Eleanor felt she learned something from that chance encounter. After all, she believed that "nothing you learn, however wide of the mark it may appear at the time, however trivial, is ever wasted."

From the time she was a young woman, Eleanor had developed a technique for engaging new people in conversation. One of her aunts had suggested the "alphabet" device to her. In her autobiography, she described it with humor as a way to make repeated and creative attempts to get someone talking. "A—Apple. Do you like apples, Mr. Smith? B—Bears. Are you afraid of bears, Mr. Jones? C—Cats. Do you have the usual feeling, Mrs. Jellyfish, about cats?" Evidently, the technique usually worked, but Eleanor encountered one spectacular failure. After sailing home from Europe in 1918, she found herself seated next to Calvin Coolidge at a luncheon in Boston. The future president sat in stony silence. Eleanor ran through the whole alphabet, but it was no use. Even she posed no match for the famously taciturn Coolidge.

Like Eleanor, you will find people who are difficult to engage. But being open to learning means making the effort to learn even in difficult situations. Your most reticent col-league, the one who appears the least willing to share her or his thoughts, may have the most interesting perspective if you take the time to seek it out. Similarly, the chance to go on that river-rafting trip or take up roller blading may be just the time to learn about how certain people work together, handle challenges, and are able to have fun.

Dynamic leadership relationships have a reciprocal heart. You must discover the hopes of others, who will, in turn, lead you into new ways of considering and acting on your vision for change. It is your ability to *"learn* from others and from the environment—the capacity *to be taught,"* according to leadership scholar James MacGregor Burns, that marks potential leadership. "That capacity calls for an ability to listen and be guided by others without being threatened by them . . . to possess enough autonomy to be creative without rejecting the external influences that make for growth and rel-evance . . . *to lead by being led."* That can only happen when you make it a habit to focus on what you can learn every day.

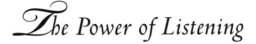

The Power of Listening

Learning is an active process that starts in a seemingly passive way—by listening. In *Leadership Is an Art,* Max De Pree writes about some South Pacific cultures where holding a conch shell symbolizes the authority of a speaker as it is passed around the group. It indicates the importance leaders place on listening to others.

Listening is the only way to work collaboratively, to build the kind of collective leadership effort that maximizes everyone's contribution. The great community organizer Saul Alinsky advised organizers to start from where people were, not from where they wanted them to be. The only way to understand where people are is to listen to their wants and needs, their hopes and frustrations, and their ideas for moving forward.

Although Eleanor spoke and wrote countless words, it was her skill for listening that gave her writing meaning and passion. She sat in crowded kitchens with small children tugging at their mothers' skirts. She sat in homes with children lying ill in bed. Sometimes the houses were so crowded that a child slept in a windowless closet with sacking for a bed. She went into the homes of miners and listened as their wives talked about their days. "Listening to such a woman talk," Eleanor wrote, "taking in the surroundings, one finds oneself, little by little, coming to understand the feelings of that other human being."

Eleanor exemplified the active listener. She used her voice and body language to show that she cared about what she was hearing. On a political trip in New York, Eleanor ended up accepting a ride with a local family in order to catch her train after a speech. The daughter, who was ten at the time, remembered almost thirty years later how Eleanor's voice sounded. "It was warm and personal. The voice of someone who was really listening to you, someone who really cared about what you said."

Looking someone in the eye, leaning toward them, nodding occasionally, and smiling are all ways to encourage others to keep talking. Having the patience to let someone finish a thought or story no matter how anxious you are to interject is a critical listening skill. Teasing out underlying meaning, feelings, and ideas by asking questions or reflecting back key points adds a powerful dimension to your listening skill.

Eleanor understood that leadership is a collaborative process, and she knew that to work together meant that people must mine the treasures of one another's skills and interests. "Along with the need for individual development," she wrote, "there is also an equally pressing need to work co-operatively. This, of course, involves learning about people and finding out how to draw the best from your association with them."

In addition to the learning that comes from involved listening, there is the attendant benefit of giving acknowledgment to the person talking. When you are an active listener, the person talking feels validated, accepted, and more willing to listen in return. Your ability to listen with intelligence and interest will spark a powerful dynamic that builds leadership on both sides of the conversation.

I learned the power of listening somewhat accidentally when I was in my twenties. I had always been interested in other people and loved to ask questions. At a job interview to be an administrative assistant, my future boss seemed rather nervous. He immediately asked me if I had any questions. I asked about the job, his children (whose pictures were on his desk), how he came to be in his position. I listened with interest, showing my attention by reflecting back some of his thoughts. By the time the interview was over he told me I was hired. As I was leaving, I realized that he had done all the talking! From then on, I used the "listening technique" in every job interview I had, and it's been consistently successful.

Whenever I meet someone new, I try to focus on spending more time listening than talking. Timing your listening is effective because often people you're talking to won't be ready to listen to you until they've had their chance to speak. Once they've had their chance, their mind will be clear to focus on what you have to say. Your ability to let them go first may actually mean that you get heard with more clarity and acceptance than if you had forged ahead. It also allows you to respond to their comments within the context of what you have to say. These same listening techniques—active listening, timing your listening, reflecting back a speaker's ideas— can be applied in group situations as well.

Eleanor talked of the powerful effect of active listening in describing her beloved Aunt Bye. Eleanor admired the older woman's graceful acceptance of her "bitter handicaps." Stricken by crippling arthritis, Bye sat confined to a chair all day, and began losing her hearing as well. Yet all the young people in the family sought her out to confide their problems and seek her wise counsel. "She had a broad understanding and a wisdom that was both sympathetic and kindly,"

Eleanor wrote. "And she had a rarer quality—she could listen. We all know the frustrating experience of trying to talk out a problem and discovering that our chosen confidant is giving us only divided attention, or frankly thinking of something else, or waiting to get in a word about some problem of his or her own." Eleanor believed that Bye was able to be a generous listener because she kept alive her curiosity and interest in new experiences.

Learn About Yourself

As you look for opportunities to learn, look inside yourself as well. Leaders who are learners are able to absorb and process information, not just acquire it. Storehouses are musty, uninviting places, and the same is true of people who gather information for the sake of the gathering. You undoubtedly know someone who is an "information-dropper" but has little self-awareness and no ability to lead. In contrast, absorbing information means integrating it into your vision and values so that it ultimately enhances your leadership skills.

If you are self-aware, you know what you don't know. Learners are by definition people who don't know everything. Leaders who are learners have the confidence to admit what they don't know. In contrast, people who are insecure don't attach appropriate value to what they do know, and feel that they should know everything. Pretending to know something because you feel you might look foolish otherwise is a sign of insecurity. If you are attending to your learning, if you are a seeker of learning and self-awareness, you can feel confident about revealing gaps in your knowledge.

Eleanor urged people to seek deeper understanding of their experiences through self-knowledge. She advised that one could only understand new experiences, "if you have arrived at some knowledge of yourself, a knowledge based on a deliberately and usually painfully acquired self-discipline, which teaches you to cast out fear and frees you for the fullest experience of the adventure of life."

But how do you arrive at knowledge of yourself? Obviously, some people do it directly with psychological counseling, but Eleanor had a different model. She sought out new challenges, going places and doing things that stretched her imagination and courage. For example, Eleanor loved to fly and took flying lessons. She respected Franklin's request that she not fly by herself, but she logged many hours as a passenger and student. One night in 1933, Eleanor climbed in next to Amelia Earhart and flew from Washington to Baltimore. Both had come from a dinner and were in their evening dresses. Earhart even kept her dress gloves on. At one point Eleanor took over flying and the plane "made a most peculiar serpentine side swing." She felt like she was on top of the world.

Being adventurous and setting up unexpected challenges is a way to learn about yourself. Like Eleanor, you can expand your horizons of personal understanding and have fun at the same time.

For me, a new challenge and adventure came when, at the age of forty-five, I took up playing soccer. I had never played a team sport before. I hadn't been an athletic girl; in fact, I had never even kicked a ball. But my friend Julie persistently asked if I would join her at a team practice, and one night I hesitantly agreed.

At that first practice, I kicked other people's shins more than the ball, and when I did kick the ball it careened wildly. I slipped and fell in the mud and thought I'd die from running so much. I also couldn't remember the last time I'd had so much fun. As I left, I had the first of many personal insights from this new adventure. I realized that the first thing I had to learn wasn't how to kick the ball, but how to stop worrying about looking foolish. I knew I looked awkward and uncoordinated, and I would for some time to come, but I consciously worked on letting go of my "looking silly" fears. That bit of personal learning has freed me in many ways, on and off the field.

In addition to the benefits of getting in shape, I've had many insights from playing soccer over the last five years. I've learned about leadership in a different context, about thinking independently and dependently almost simultaneously as the game requires, about meshing skills to maximize success and, most important, about the force of women's support for each other.

That support hit home when I joined a women's over-thirty team. The team members came from different backgrounds and mostly knew only a little about one another's lives. We were there to play soccer. Toward the end of that first season, I somehow ended up in the forward line during a game where my team was comfortably ahead. Miraculously, the ball found my foot and went into the goal. You would have thought my teammates had won a million dollars each. I couldn't remember seeing such unbridled joy over someone else's accomplishment. That day I learned something else about myself—how much I valued my bonds with other women, how much I valued being part of a team.

Pass It On

For three weeks during her travels in the spring of 1952, Eleanor's "My Day" column read like a travelogue. From New Delhi she wrote, "We saw one of the hill tribesmen who had spent the winter down in this warmer area and was on his homeward trek. He had probably lived on the sand in one of those odd little round huts they build with bent bamboo ribs and which open out like a folding basket to hold up the outside . . . . The faces of the people are extraordinary and their carriage is regal in its dignity for both men and women . . . ." From Bombay, "So far India means color to me—brilliant color in cotton saris, in silk saris, and in beautiful embroideries so vivid that perhaps at home they would look out of place . . . . We drove through a slum area on the way back . . . . The streets are cleaned by people using little straw brooms—just a few sticks tied together—and the sweepers scrape up every bit of dirt into tin containers." From Katmandu, in Nepal, "I have just learned that I was in error earlier this month when I called the memorial to Gandhi in New Delhi his tomb. This was incorrect as, according to custom, his body was cremated and the ashes were buried in the Ganges. The Indian name for the memorial we visited is Samadhi."

Eleanor wrote her columns as a way of teaching what she was learning. She wanted to bring about an understanding between nations. Such an understanding, she believed, held the key to peace for the world. "I cannot overemphasize how essential it is that we show respect for the customs of people from foreign countries, and particularly people from different cultures and environments," she wrote.

Experience had taught her that understanding came in small ways—from appreciating different lifestyles and rituals, from respecting different customs and values. Her "My Day" readers were more than an audience for her public diary, they were citizens who could help influence changes that Eleanor hoped to see in her own country. She saw a duty to teach what she had learned, to "pass it on" so that others would work with her and also become leaders for change.

Eleanor's communication about her own learning also communicated that learning itself had value. Eleanor showed Americans that she found excitement in new experiences. She demonstrated her respect for other cultures and modeled humility and openness about little-known people and places. She was teaching others to be learners like herself.

Teaching by deeds as well as words became natural to Eleanor. While she welcomed the chance to learn new customs, such as how to use chopsticks, she drew the line at practices that violated her values, and often she would demonstrate her disapproval with actions rather than words. One day, while in Japan, Eleanor took a walk with a man and his wife. She knew and disapproved of the practice of women walking several steps behind their husbands. As she walked with the wife, she made sure that they kept up with the woman's husband. "In this way," Eleanor wrote, "without any comment or criticism, I made it clear that this was a custom which, to the Westerner, seemed to indicate a disrespect for women which we could not condone or accept."

Eleanor showed that the power of learning will most directly be felt in one's ability to teach what he or she has learned. This doesn't mean lecturing, standing up with a ruler, and spouting information. Leaders who teach translate their learning in ways that motivate others. They turn their experiences outward in service to their vision. They model through words and actions the leadership they have learned and the leadership they hope to see in others.

There is a vibrant interplay between learning leaders and those they teach. It shows up as new learning takes place, as new ideas are exchanged, and as new leaders emerge. Eleanor, passionate learner, teacher, and leader wrote with timeless truth about the learning role leaders must take. "Never, perhaps, have any of us needed as much as we do today to use all the curiosity we have, needed to seek new knowledge, needed to realize that no knowledge is terminal. For almost everything in our world is new, startlingly new . . . . Each new bit of knowledge, each new experience is an extra tool in meeting new problems and working them out."

Eleanor wrote these words more than four decades ago. Now it is your turn to learn, to teach, and to lead.

ELEANOR'S WAY

- Learn from everyone by inviting others to teach you.

- Give any new idea a few minutes of your time. You never know what you can learn or how your leadership will be enhanced.

- Be curious. Curiosity nurtures the souls and spirits of people.

- Keep your organization and your brain healthy by offering challenge and revelation.

- Learn and listen. Leaders who are the best learners are the best listeners.

- Empower others by honoring their ideas with your serious attention and interest.

- Be a leader who is a learner; be a learner who is a teacher; be a teacher who is a leader who motivates others to lead and learn.

- Find the fun in learning, and spend time learning some things that are fun.

- Discover things about yourself that will add to your confidence and competence as a leader.

Epilogue

*I*n 1952, when Dwight D. Eisenhower became the first Republican in twenty years to be elected president, he ended Eleanor's term as a United Nations delegate. She had campaigned for his rival, Adlai Stevenson, and supposedly made disparaging comments about Eisenhower's wife's drinking problems. Eleanor moved over to a nongovernmental organization called the American Association for the United Nations (AAUN) and continued to be an unofficial ambassador of the United States. She visited the emperor in Japan, made a painful visit to Hiroshima, where Truman had dropped the first atomic bomb, and visited Yugoslavian leader Marshal Tito on the island of Brioni. Stating the obvious, Eleanor told Emma Bugbee of the *Herald-Tribune*, "I have not slackened my pace."

On the eve of Eleanor's seventieth birthday in 1954, Herbert Block penned a cartoon that captured the former first lady's place in the nation's imagination. From the deck of a large ship a mother, surrounded by suitcases, bends over her daughter. The woman is looking at the girl as she smiles and points to the Statue of Liberty looming in the distance. The caption has the excited child telling her mother, "Of course I know—it's Mrs. Roosevelt."

Eleanor celebrated her birthday with a fund-raiser for the AAUN. She looked radiantly happy. Her gray hair, now tinged with white, was swept up on either side, and her pale full-skirted gown accented her elegance. When she rose to speak, the audience no doubt recognized the "odd fluting yet precise voice with its careful emphases, its nervous glissade of giggles," as the author Gore Vidal had described her. She spoke of the satisfaction she got from her work at the U.N., the need for its continuance, her hopes for peace. Summing up her seven decades she said, "Life has got to be lived, that's all there is to it."

Between her travels, Eleanor lived out her last years at her beloved Val-Kill. The woodsy retreat served as a staging area for Eleanor's projects. In the 1950s she fought the anti-Communist hysteria marked by the House Un-American Activities Committee and its bullying chairman, Joseph McCarthy. She campaigned a second time for Adlai Stevenson in 1956. Dusting herself off after the hard-fought campaign, she traveled to Morocco, started writing a new book, and worked within the Democratic Party to win back those who had voted for Eisenhower.

In between travels to Israel, the Philippines, Hong Kong, and Indonesia, Eleanor entertained her grandchildren by the stream and in the pool at Val-Kill. Eleanor belly-flopped into the water, paddling with strength if not grace. She quickly shifted from homey activities such as knitting to penning answers to the questions posed in her monthly column for *McCall's Magazine*. As always, her correspondence flowed in and out in an endless tide. The woman who was a brilliant guest on *Meet the Press* caught a visitor by surprise one day when he found her kneeling before the toilet bowl at Val-Kill arranging gladiolas. She sheepishly explained that this was her secret for keeping them fresh.

Politics held Eleanor's attention. Her stride reduced to a shuffle, she attended the 1960 Democratic nominating convention in Los Angeles. She pushed for a Stevenson-Kennedy ticket, but the young, vibrant New Englander carried off the presidential nomination on the first ballot. Eleanor said the political battle had been a good fight that she enjoyed. Then she held off her endorsement of Kennedy until he assured her that Adlai Stevenson would be well-placed in a Kennedy White House. Once again Eleanor followed her old rule: If you have to compromise, "compromise up." Once assured that she had Kennedy's ear, Eleanor campaigned for him with vigor. She used her column to applaud his abilities, she spoke on his behalf and, not surprisingly, she gave him political and policy advice. She remained an adviser and more once Kennedy took office. He placed her on the council for the Peace Corps and asked her to chair his Commission on the Status of Women.

Eleanor's commitment to racial equality still animated her life. Her first guest on her television show, *The Prospects of Mankind*, was civil rights leader Martin Luther King, Jr. When King was jailed in Georgia in 1962 for marching to protest segregationist policies, Eleanor wrote on his behalf to attorney general Robert Kennedy. Kennedy's aides managed to get the charges against King and the other protesters dropped, no doubt at least in part due to Eleanor's influence.

In September 1962, Eleanor began to succumb to the fever, exhaustion, and pain that had plagued her throughout the year. She was hospitalized and hated it, falling into depression and fighting off the effects of horrible dreams. She told friends that she was ready to die. Eleanor returned home and tried to continue work on her book, *Tomorrow Is Now*, a passionate plea for world peace and understanding, but her temperature rose again, and an angry, helpless Eleanor went back to the hospital. She finally returned home one last time, as a rare bone-marrow tuberculosis slowly ended her life. On November 7, 1962, Eleanor Roosevelt died. She was buried by her husband's side in an oak casket draped with fir boughs in the Rose Garden at Hyde Park on the tenth of November.

At the funeral, President Kennedy and his wife stood alongside vice president Lyndon Johnson and every former president except Hoover, who was too ill to travel. Hundreds of friends and relatives, who had overwhelmed the service at St. James Church, found the town of Hyde Park shuttered in mourning. From that hamlet on the Hudson River the grief of those who came to mourn was echoed around the world. Eleanor had touched literally thousands of people's lives, had created lasting change on a global scale, and had brought her leadership to countless causes.

She would be sorely missed, but her legacy would carry forward. Even today she is called "First Lady of the World."

"I Want You to Write to Me"

*W*hen Eleanor started writing for *The Women's Home Companion* magazine in 1933, she used the title on this page for her first column. She explained that she wanted to help as many people as she could with their problems, but she also wanted people to help each other by sharing their experiences.

If this book has inspired your thinking about leadership and your life, as I hope it has, I would like to hear from you. What is your *leadership way*? What are the best leadership lessons you know, and the stories behind them? In the spirit of Eleanor Roosevelt, perhaps we can help each other.

You can write to me at:

Robin Gerber
Academy of Leadership
1108 Talliaferro Hall
College Park, MD 20742

Or email to:

eleanor@academy.umd.edu

Notes

Book Abbreviations in Notes

E&F—Eleanor and Franklin, Joseph Lash
TIMS—This Is My Story, Eleanor Roosevelt
YLBL—You Learn by Living, Eleanor Roosevelt
TIR—This I Remember, Eleanor Roosevelt
OMO—On My Own, Eleanor Roosevelt

(Full citations are contained in the bibliography.)

Introduction

Anderson concert from Black, *Casting Her Shadow,* and Black, "Championing a Champion: Eleanor Roosevelt and the Marian Anderson 'Freedom Concert,'" *Presidential Studies Quarterly* 20, no. 4 (Fall 1990); Howard Gardner from *Leading Minds;* Margaret Wheatley from *Turning to One Another;* for statistics on women in business see "The Committee of 200 Annual Report on Women's Clout in Business 2002," the Government Accounting Office Report "Women in Management," article at womensenews.org/

article.cfm/dyn/aid/796/, web site for the Center for American Women and Politics at Rutgers University: www.rci.rutgers. edu/~cawp/.

Chapter One: Learn from Your Past

Eleanor's early leadership from Lash, *E&F*; on creating a grass-roots movement from Cook II, "overcome obstacles" quote, ER, *Autobiography*; "I must have been," *TIMS*, "one of the most beautiful," TIMS; "I was a solemn child," ER, ed. *Hunting Big Game in the Eighties*; "I can remember," *TIMS*; "I simply refused," *TIMS*; "I was an exceptionally," ER, *YLBL*; Burns quote from *Leadership*; "You must try to understand truthfully," ER, *YLBL*; Mulcahy story, *Wall Street Journal*, October 10, 2001; "This power of imagination," ER, *YLBL*; "one's childhood," *TIMS*; J. W. Gardner quote from *Morale*; "In her personal struggle," from Lash, *Life Was Meant to Be Lived*.

Chapter Two: Find Mentors and Advisers

"All my life," ER, "The Seven People Who Shaped My Life," *Look*, 1951; "Your mother wanted you to go to boarding school," Lash, *E&F*; "Thus, the second period," *TIMS*; "lost and very lonely," *TIMS*; "short and rather stout," *TIMS*; "the purity of Eleanor's heart," letter in FDR Library, Hyde Park;

"Women of Color Executives: Their Voices, Their Journeys," Catalyst study, 2001; "What you are in life," ER and Black, *What I Hope to Leave Behind,* p. 39; "a passionate humanist," from Cook I; "I have seen," *TIMS*; on ER's overall personal change at Allenswood see Cook I; ER's health and physical activity, *TIMS*; Alassio story, *TIMS*; "Mlle. Souvestre had become one of the people," *TIMS*.

Chapter Three: Mothering: Training for Leadership

"Remember that a home," ER and Black, *What I Hope to Leave Behind*; "In return for the privilege," Lash, *E&F*; "I was beginning to be an entirely dependent person," *TIMS*; "One thing I've personally experienced," Sumru Erkut, *Inside Women's Power: Learning from Leaders*, Wellesley College Center for Research on Women and Winds of Change Foundation, 2001; "warmly like a mom," ibid; "for leaders who are women of color," ibid; "I left everything," *TIMS*; "To this day," *TIMS*; "if you can manage a group of small children," *Inside Women's Power: Learning from Leaders*; "Ethics of Parents" (unpublished article) in Lash, *E&F*; "a small army on the march," Lash, *E&F*; "I've paid 60 calls in Washington," Lash, *E&F*; "My time was now completely filled," *TIMS*; "My first obligaton," TIMS; "Eleanor Roosevelt has five children," Lash, *E&F*.

Chapter Four: Learning the Hard Way

"Readjustment is a kind of private revolution," ER, *YLBL*; "It was not an unusual thing," *TIMS*; Lucy Mercer story see Jonathan Daniels, *The Washington Quadrille: The Dance Beside the Documents*, Garden City, NY, Doubleday,1968; "the same brand of charm," Elliott Roosevelt and James Brough, *An Untold Story: The Roosevelts of Hyde Park*, NY, Putnam, 1973; "I saw you 20 miles out in the country," Michael Teague, *Mrs. L: Conversations with Alice Roosevelt Longworth*, Garden City, NY, Doubleday, 1981; "The bottom dropped out of my own particular world," Lash, *E&F*; "Nothing ever happens to us," ER, *YLBL*; "looking like a stringbean," Lash, *E&F*; "Periods of isolation," Howard Gardner from *Leading Minds*; ER quotes from European trip and Grandmother Hall's death from *TIMS*; ER quotes on courage and disaster from ER, *YLBL*; Margaret Wheatley from *Turning to One Another*; ER on readjusting from ER, *YLBL*.

Chapter Five: Find Your Leadership Passion

"Work is easier," ER, *YLBL*; Eleanor's activism in the 1920s, Cook I; "I think in some of us there is an urge," from *My Day*; Maslow from *Motivation and Personality*; "The world is moved," John W. Gardner from *On Leadership*; onset of FDR's polio from Lash, *E&F*, and Burns, *Roosevelt: The Lion and the Fox*; "Give your reason for or against allowing women," from

Lash, *E&F*; ER's life at Val-Kill from Cook I; "I teach because I love it," Black, *Courage in a Dangerous World*; "Walking was so difficult for him," *TIR*; "If we are still a negligible factor," ER, "Women Must Learn to Play the Game as Men Do," *Redbook* magazine, 1928.

Chapter Six: Your Leadership Your Way

"Women, whether subtly or vociferously," ER, *It's Up to the Women*; "I never wanted to be a President's wife," Lash, *E&F*; "She had a following," Cook I; "to do things on my own," Black, *Casting Her Own Shadow*; Rita Halle story, Cook I; Arthurdale experiment, Lash, *E&F*; "Trial by Fire: A Tale of Gender and Leadership," Carol Becker, *Chronicle of Higher Education*, 1/25/02; "She shattered the ceremonial mold," Goodwin, *No Ordinary Time*; "a feeling that you have been honest," ER, *YLBL*; "the radical end of New Deal thinking," Cook II.

Chapter Seven: Give Voice to Your Leadership

"If you have something to say," Lash *E&F*; women-only press conferences from Beasley, *Eleanor Roosevelt and the Media*, "She's got a message," Lash, *E&F*; Bennis from *Leaders*; "flood of correspondence," Black, *Casting Her Own Shadow*; Bess Truman story from George Martin, *Madame Secretary*, Boston:

Houghton Mifflin Company, 1976; bonus army story from Lash, *E&F*; "there was a dime's worth of difference," Cook II.

Chapter Eight: Face Criticism with Courage

"Develop a skin," Cook I from *Democratic Digest*, 1936; Junior League story, Lash, *E&F*; stories on ER's travels from Wolfskill; "To be really constructive," "How to Take Criticism," *Ladies Home Journal*, November, 1944; Cobell story in *Parade* magazine, September 9, 2001; "She has gone out," Lash, *E&F*; "It was one of the occasions," *The Autobiography of Eleanor Roosevelt*; "have ever been subjected to personal abuse," Adlai Stevenson eulogy at Memorial Service, New York City, November 17, 1962; "As time went by I found that people," *The Autobiography of Eleanor Roosevelt*; "Do what you feel in your heart to be right," "How to Take Criticism" (see above); "Because she stood her ground," H. Gardner, *Leading Minds*; "Most black people were struck," Vernon Jarrett from *The American Experience*, PBS.

Chapter Nine: Keep Your Focus

"To be useful," ER, *YLBL*; "Right wing zealots," Wolfskill and Hudson, *All But the People*; Perkins impeachment story, George Martin, *Madame Secretary*, Boston: Houghton Mifflin Company, 1976; "tumult of 50,000," Lash, *E&F*; "ER's commitment to racial justice," Black, *Casting Her Own Shadow*;

"May what is best for the country," *My Day*, 1940; "living here is very oppressive," Bernard Asbell, *Mother and Daughter: The Letters of Eleanor and Anna Roosevelt*, New York, Fromm, 1988; "you must do the thing," ER, *YLBL*; "It was the New Deal social objectives," *TIR*; Tugwell quoted in Lash, *E&F*; "Soon I will expect Sistie and Buzzy," Jean Nienaber Clarke, *Roosevelt's Warrior, Harold L. Ickes and the New Deal*, Baltimore, The Johns Hopkins University Press, 1996; Eleanor's views on national defense, Lash, *E&F*; Odell Waller story, Lash, *E&F*, Black, *Casting Her Own Shadow*; on racial equality in the military and women in the military, Goodwin, *No Ordinary Time*; "Surely, in the light of history," ER, *YLBL*.

Chapter Ten: Contacts, Networks, and Connections

"Human relationships, like life itself," ER, *YLBL*; "unusually smart," Asbell, *Mother and Daughter* (chapter nine); "Harry, the President is dead," David McCullough, *Truman*, New York, Touchstone, 1992; "always just getting over," *TIMS*; "Women must become more conscious," *Good Housekeeping* magazine, 1940; "I hope you will remember," Martin, *Madame Secretary* (chapter nine); "to checkmate," *New York Times*, 1924; "The narrower you make the circle," ER, *YLBL*; "Mummie's strange friends," ER, *YLBL*; "We older people," "Facing the Problems of Youth," *National Parent-Teacher Magazine*, 1935.

Chapter Eleven: Embrace Risk

"What matters now, as always," ER, *YLBL*; "heavyhearted at the thought," ER, *OMO*; "Oh, no! It would be impossible," *OMO*; Eleanor's selection for Committee Three and Vishinsky debate from Glendon; "A study in 2001," "What Women Want in Business: Power, Money and Influence—Why Women Executives Leave Corporate America for Entrepreneurial Ventures," study by Korn/Ferry International, Columbia Business School and the Duran Group; "Obviously it requires effort to use your potentialities," ER, *YLBL*; "It is true that I am fundamentally an optimist," ER, *YLBL*; "tough-minded optimism," J. W. Gardner, *On Leadership*; Eleanor's prayer from Glendon; "the frailties and sins," Maslow; "Many of us thought that lack of standards," ER, *Foreign Affairs*, 1948; "exchange roles over time," Burns, *Leadership*.

Chapter Twelve: Never Stop Learning

"Today, living and learning," ER, *YLBL*; Eleanor at the Taj Mahal Hotel from *Time* magazine, 1952; "bustling back and forth," ER, *Autobiography*; "the sword of partition," ER, *Autobiography*; "I have come to learn," Lash, *Eleanor: The Years Alone*; "You must be interested in anything," ER, *YLBL*; "learn from others and from the environment," Burns, *Leadership*; "It was warm and personal," Hershan; "she had a broad understanding," ER, *YLBL*; "if you have arrived at some knowledge," ER, *YLBL*; "Never, perhaps, have any of us needed," ER, *YLBL*.

Resources

*Where to Go to Find More Information
About Eleanor Roosevelt*

The American Experience: Eleanor Roosevelt
http://www.pbs.org/wgbh/amex/eleanor
This site describes and enhances the *American Experience* film
Eleanor Roosevelt with a program description, interviews, parts
of Eleanor's FBI file, the Roosevelt family tree, reprints of her
daily syndicated "My Day" column, a clip from her television
program, her life timeline, an interactive version of "Eleanor's
Tour" through the South Pacific, information on people fea-
tured in the film, and even a teacher's guide.

Eleanor Roosevelt Center at Val-Kill
http://www.ervk.org
(845) 229-5302
ERVK
P.O. Box 255
Hyde Park, New York 12538
Eleanor Roosevelt Center at Val-Kill is a nonpartisan, non-
profit organization dedicated to Eleanor Roosevelt's belief

that people can enhance the quality of their lives through purposeful action based on sensitive discourse among people of diverse perspectives focusing on the varied needs of society.

Eleanor Roosevelt National Historic Site
http://www.nps.gov/elro
(845) 229-9115
Eleanor Roosevelt National Historic Site
4097 Albany Post Road
Hyde Park, NY 12538
Maintained by the National Park Service, this site describes Eleanor Roosevelt's home in Hyde Park, which she called Val-Kill. Here, one can find information on travel, fees, activities, and other aspects of visiting the only National Historic Site dedicated to a first lady.

The Eleanor Roosevelt Papers
http://www.gwu.edu/~erpapers
(202) 242-6717
The Eleanor Roosevelt Papers
The George Washington University at Mount Vernon College
2100 Foxhall Road, NW
Washington, DC 20007
The Eleanor Roosevelt Papers is the first phase of the Eleanor Roosevelt and Human Rights Project and offers a documentary history of Eleanor Roosevelt's political writings and radio and television appearances. Many of Eleanor Roosevelt's political writings in print and electronic format can be found here.

Franklin and Eleanor Roosevelt Institute
http://www.newdeal.feri.org/feri
Franklin and Eleanor Roosevelt Institute
4079 Albany Post Road
Hyde Park, NY 12538
The mission of the Roosevelt Institute is to inform new generations of the ideals and achievements of Franklin and Eleanor Roosevelt and to inspire the application of their spirit of optimism and innovation to the solution of current problems. The site contains links to other Roosevelt sites such as the International Roosevelt Resource Centers and the Roosevelt Study Center.

Franklin D. Roosevelt Library and Museum
http://www.fdrlibrary.marist.edu
(845) 229-8114
The Museum of the Franklin D. Roosevelt Library
4079 Albany Post Road
Hyde Park, New York 12538
These digital archives give the general public access to a portion of documents, photographs, sound and video recordings, finding aids, and other primary source materials found at the Franklin D. Roosevelt Library, which include a wealth of information about Eleanor Roosevelt.

The National Women's History Project

http://www.nwhp.org

(707) 636-2888

The National Women's History Project

3343 Industrial Drive, Suite 4

Santa Rosa, CA 95403

The National Women's History Project is an educational non-profit organization for recognition and celebration of the diverse and historic accomplishments of women. It offers current information about women who have actively sought to improve the status of women in society both in the United States and around the world.

New Deal Network

http://www.newdeal.feri.org

(212) 678-4161

New Deal Network

Institute for Learning Technologies

Teachers College/Columbia University

525 W. 120th St. Box 144

New York, NY 10027

The New Deal Network is an educational guide to the Great Depression in the 1930s sponsored by the Franklin and Eleanor Roosevelt Institute and the Institute for Learning Technologies. Here, one can search through a document library and a photo gallery, and even peruse letters written from American children to Eleanor Roosevelt during the Depression, including her responses to their pleas for help.

The Universal Declaration of Human Rights
http://www.udhr.org
(212) 259-1259
Michael Cooper
Representative to the United Nations
Franklin and Eleanor Roosevelt Institute
350 Fifth Avenue, 34th Floor
New York, NY 10118
The Franklin and Eleanor Roosevelt Institute celebrates and promotes Eleanor's work with the Universal Declaration of Human Rights. Here, a biographical profile and transcripts of articles and speeches given by Eleanor on human rights can be found.

Where to Go to Find More Information About Women's Leadership

Anthony Center for Women's Leadership
http://www.rochester.edu/SBA
(585) 275-8799
Anthony Center for Women's Leadership
University of Rochester
RC Box 270435
Rochester, NY 14627-0435
The center continues the fight for women's full social, political, and economic equality, and encourages all to understand and overcome barriers to women's leadership. The site

boasts programs and events listings, resources and links, women's suffrage history, and more.

Catalyst

http://www.catalystwomen.org

(212) 514-7600

Catalyst is a nonprofit research and advisory organization working to advance women in business and the professions, with offices in New York, California, and Toronto. The group has been a leading source of information on women in business for the past four decades.

Center for American Women and Politics

http://iwl.rutgers.edu/cawp.htm

(732) 932-9384

Center for American Women and Politics

Eagleton Institute of Politics

Rutgers, The State University of New Jersey

191 Ryders Lane

New Brunswick, NJ 08901-8557

CAWP's mission is to promote greater understanding and knowledge about women's relationships to politics and government, and to enhance women's influence and leadership in public life. The center conducts programs for women public officials, does research on the impact of women in public life, runs educational programs that connect students to the world of policy makers, and offers residential institutes for college women.

Center for Women's Global Leadership

http://www.cwgl.rutgers.edu

(732) 932-8782

Center for Women's Global Leadership

Douglass College

Rutgers, The State University of New Jersey

160 Ryders Lane

New Brunswick, NJ 08901-8555

The center develops and facilitates women's leadership for women's human rights and social justice worldwide. This site contains news, articles, resources, publications, and links concerning women's leadership and women's rights.

International Center for Research on Women

http://www.icrw.org

(202) 797-0007

International Center for Research on Women

1717 Massachusetts Avenue, NW, Suite 302

Washington, DC 20036

Named one of the nation's top charities, ICRW's mission is to improve the lives of women in poverty, advance women's equality and human rights, and contribute to broader economic and social well-being. ICRW accomplishes this, in partnership with others, through research, capacity building, and advocacy.

National Council of Women's Organizations
http://www.womensorganizations.org
(202) 393-7122
National Council of Women's Organizations
733 15th St. NW, Suite 1011
Washington, DC 20005
The council is composed of more than one hundred organizations working on issues such as equal employment opportunity; economic equity and development; education; and job training.

UNIFEM
http://www.undp.org/unifem
(212) 906-6400
United Nations Development Fund for Women
304 East 45th Street, 15th floor
New York, NY 10017
UNIFEM promotes women's empowerment and gender equality and works to ensure the participation of women in all levels of development planning and practice. UNIFEM supports efforts that link the needs and concerns of women to all critical issues on the national, regional, and global agendas.

Vital Voices Global Partnership
http://gw.vitalvoices.org/node/237231
(202) 772-4162
Vital Voices Global Partnership
1050 Connecticut Ave., NW 10th Floor
Washington, DC 20036

A worldwide nongovernmental organization of women leaders devoted to the economic, social, and political progress of women around the world, Vital Voices works to expand women's roles in politics and civil society, increase successful women's entrepreneurship, and fight human rights abuses. The site contains information on the partnership's Afghan women's leadership program, the Vital Voices Global Leadership Institute at Georgetown University, various activities and news, and a stance to stop trafficking in women and girls.

Wellesley Centers for Women
http://www.wellesley.edu/WCW/crwsub.html
(781) 283-2500
Wellesley Centers for Women
Wellesley College
106 Central Street
Wellesley, MA 02481
An alliance of the Stone Center and the Center for Research on Women at Wellesley College, the Wellesley Centers for Women is the nation's largest women's research center. Its interdisciplinary community of scholars focuses on research, training, analysis, and action to help create a world that is better for women.

The White House Project
http://thewhitehouseproject.org
(212) 785-6001
White House Project
110 Wall Street, 2nd Floor
New York, NY 10005
The White House Project/Women's Leadership Fund is a national, nonpartisan organization dedicated to advancing women's leadership by enhancing public perceptions of women's capacity to lead and fostering the entry of women into positions of leadership, including the U.S. presidency. The White House Project achieves these goals through research, public education campaigns, measures to influence popular culture, and forums to heighten women's visibility.

Women's EDGE
http://www.womensedge.org
(202) 884-8396
Women's EDGE
1825 Connecticut Avenue NW, Suite 800
Washington, DC 20009
Women's EDGE is a dynamic coalition of individuals and respected organizations that is giving women and families around the world an economic edge. The site lists programs, resources, events, publications, and information on their GAINS for Women and Girls campaign.

Women's Enews
http://womensenews.org
(212) 244-1720
Women's Enews
146 W. 29th Street, 7R
New York, NY 10001
A nonprofit independent news service, Women's Enews covers issues that are of particular concern to women. The site contains various daily articles, a searchable archive for the last ninety days, and even a sources database.

Women's International Center
http://www.wic.org
(619) 295-6446
Women's International Center
P.O. Box 880736
San Diego, CA 92168-0736
WIC celebrates women and their positive, enduring contributions to humanity through its annual Living Legacy Awards honoring women, its educational home at the Women's International Institute, and its permanent home at the WIC, displaying the enduring works of women in museums, theaters, and in WIC's Women's Hall of Humanity.

Women's Leadership Development Program

http://www.ipa.udel.edu/wldp

(302) 831-8971

Women's Leadership Development Program

Institute for Public Administration

180 Graham Hall

University of Delaware

Newark, DE 19716

The program provides opportunities for women in public service to improve and develop their leadership skills so they can become more effective in the various roles in which they are involved. It focuses on individual development and is based on the belief that individuals can expand their leadership capacities.

Women's Research and Education Institute

http://www.wrei.org

(202) 628-0444

Women's Research and Education Institute

1750 New York Avenue, NW, Suite 350

Washington, DC 20006

A respected resource for legislators, administrators, state and local government officials, women's advocates, corporate policy makers, the media, teachers, students and more, WREI's mission is to identify issues affecting women and their roles in the family, workplace, and public arena, and to inform and help shape the public policy debate on these issues.

Bibliography

The following are books on leadership and related themes that were used in writing *Leadership: the Eleanor Roosevelt Way.*

Ambrose, Delorese. *Leadership: The Journey Inward* (Dubuque, Iowa: Kendall/Hunt Publishing, 1991), 2nd ed.

Astin, Helen and Carole Leland. *Women of Influence Women of Vision* (San Francisco: Jossey-Bass Publishers, 1991).

Bennis, Warren and Burt Nanus. *Leaders* (New York: HarperCollins, 1985).

Book, Esther Wachs. *Why the Best Man for the Job Is a Woman: The Unique Female Qualities of Leadership* (New York: HarperCollins, 2000).

Burns, James MacGregor. *Leadership* (New York: HarperCollins, 1978).

Chrislip, David D. and Carl E. Larson. *Collaborative Leadership: How Citizens and Civic Leaders Make a Difference* (San Francisco: Jossey-Bass Publishers, 1999).

Clifton, Donald O. and Paula Nelson. *Soar with Your Strengths* (New York: Dell Publishing, 1992).

Cook, Blanche Wiesen. *Eleanor Roosevelt, vol. 1, 1883–1933* (New York: Viking, 1992).

———. *Eleanor Roosevelt, vol. 2, 1933–1938* (New York: Viking, 1999).

Crittenden, Ann. *The Price of Motherhood: Why the Most Important Job in the World Is Still the Least Valued* (New York: Metropolitan Books, Henry Holt and Company, 2001).

De Pree, Max. *Leadership Is an Art* (East Lansing, Michigan: Michigan State University Press, 1987).

Evans, Gail. *Play Like a Man, Win Like a Women: What Men Know About Success That Women Need to Learn* (New York: Broadway Books, 2000).

Freeman, Sue J. M., Susan C. Bourque, and Christine M. Shelton, eds. *Women on Power: Leadership Redefined* (Boston: Northeastern University Press, 2001).

Gardner, Howard. *Leading Minds: An Anatomy of Leadership* (New York: BasicBooks, 1995).

Gardner, John W. *Morale* (New York: W.W. Norton and Company, Inc., 1978).

———. *On Leadership* (New York: The Free Press, Inc., 1990).

Gilligan, Carol. *In a Different Voice: Psychological Theory and Women's Development.* (Cambridge, Massachusetts: Harvard University Press, 1982).

Gladwell, Malcolm. *The Tipping Point: How Little Things Make a Big Difference* (Boston: Little Brown and Company, 2000).

Goodwin, Doris Kearns. *No Ordinary Time* (New York: Simon & Schuster, 1994).

Greenleaf, Robert K. *Servant Leadership: A Journey into the Nature of Legitimate Power and Greatness* (New York: Paulist Press, 1977).

Handlin, Amy H. *Whatever Happened to the Year of the Woman? Why Women Still Aren't Making It to the Top in Politics* (Denver: Arden Press, 1998).

Heifetz, Ronald A. *Leadership Without Easy Answers* (Cambridge, Massachusetts: Belknap Press, 1994).

Helgesen, Sally. *The Female Advantage: Women's Ways of Leading* (New York: Doubleday, 1990).

Hershan, Stella K. *The Candles She Lit: The Legacy of Eleanor Roosevelt* (New York: Praeger, 1993).

Hickman, Gill Robinson, ed. *Leading Organizations: Perspectives for a New Era* (Thousand Oaks, California: SAGE Publications, 1998).

Kanter, Rosabeth Moss. *Men and Women of the Corporation.* (New York: BasicBooks, 1977).

Klenke, Karin. *Women and Leadership: A Contextual Perspective* (New York: Springer Publishing Company, Inc., 1996).

Komives, Susan R., Lycois Lucas, Nance and Timothy R. McMahon. *Exploring Leadership: For College Students Who Want to Make a Difference* (San Francisco: Jossey-Bass Publishers, 1998).

Kouzes, James M. and Barry Z. Posner. *The Leadership Challenge* (San Francisco: Jossey-Bass Publishers, 1995).

Kotter, John P. *John P. Kotter on What Leaders Really Do* (Boston: A Harvard Business Review Book, 1999).

Lipman-Blumen, Jean. *The Connective Edge: Leading in an Interdependent World* (San Francisco: Jossey-Bass Publishers, Inc., 1996).

——. *Gender Roles and Power* (Upper Saddle River, New Jersey: Prentice-Hall Inc., 1984).

Mackoff, Barbara and Gary Wenet. *The Inner Work of Leaders: Leadership as a Habit of the Mind.* (New York: AMACOM, 2001).

Maslow, Abraham H. *Motivation and Personality* (New York: Harper and Row Publishers, Inc., 1954).

Matusak, Larraine R. *Finding Your Voice* (San Francisco: Jossey-Bass Publishers, 1997).

Morrison, Ann M. *The New Leaders: Leadership Diversity in America* (San Francisco: Jossey-Bass Publishers, 1992).

——, Randall P. White, Ellen Van Velsor. *Breaking the Glass Ceiling: Can Women Reach the Top of America's Largest Corporations?* (Cambridge, Massachusetts: Perseus Press, 1994).

Pearson, Carol S. *The Hero Within: Six Archetypes We Live By* (San Francisco: Harper & Row, 1989).

Phillips, Donald T. *Lincoln on Leadership: Executive Strategies for Tough Times* (New York: Warner Books, 1992).

Rosener, Judy B. *America's Competitive Secret: Women Managers* (New York: Oxford University Press, 1995).

——. "Ways Women Lead." *Harvard Business Review*, November–December 1990.

Senge, Peter M. *The Fifth Discipline: The Art & Practice of the Learning Organization* (New York: Currency Doubleday, 1990).

Wheatley, Margaret J. *Turning to One Another: Simple Conversations to Restore Hope to the Future* (San Francisco: Berrett-Koehler Publishers, Inc., 2002).

White, Kate. *Why Good Girls Don't Get Ahead . . . But Gutsy Girls Do: 9 Secrets Every Working Woman Must Know* (New York: Warner Books, Inc., 1995).

Witherspoon, Patricia D. *Communicating Leadership: An Organizational Perspective* (Boston: Allyn & Bacon, 1996).

Wren, J. Thomas, ed. *The Leader's Companion: Insights on Leadership Through the Ages* (New York: The Free Press, 1995).

The following are biographies and other historical works that were used in writing this book:

Asbell, Bernard. *Mother and Daughter: The Letters of Eleanor and Anna Roosevelt* (New York: Fromm, 1988).

Beasley, Maurine H. *Eleanor Roosevelt and the Media* (Urbana: University of Illinois Press, 1987).

———, Holly C. Shulman and Henry R. Beasley. *The Encyclopedia of Eleanor Roosevelt.* (Westport, Connecticut: Greenwood Press, 2001).

Black, Allida M. *Casting Her Own Shadow: Eleanor Roosevelt and the Shaping of Postwar Liberalism* (New York: Columbia University Press, 1996).

———. *Courage in a Dangerous World: The Political Writings of Eleanor Roosevelt* (New York: Columbia University Press, 1999).

———. *What I Hope to Leave Behind: The Essential Essays of Eleanor Roosevelt* (Brooklyn, NY: Carlson Publishing, Inc., 1995).

Burns, James MacGregor. *Roosevelt: The Lion and the Fox* (New York: Harcourt, Brace & World, Inc., 1956).

———. *Roosevelt: The Soldier of Freedom* (New York: Harcout Brace Jovanovich, Inc., 1970).

Burns, James MacGregor and Susan Dunn. *The Three Roosevelts: Patrician Leaders Who Transformed America* (New York: Atlantic Monthly Press, 2001).

Collier, Peter. *The Roosevelts: An American Saga* (New York: Simon & Schuster, 1994).

Cook, Blanche Wiesen. *Eleanor Roosevelt: Volume 1* (New York: Penguin Books USA Inc., 1992).

——. *Eleanor Roosevelt: Volume 2* (New York: Viking, 1999).

Daniels, Jonathon. *Washington Quadrille: The Dance Beside the Documents* (Garden City, New York: Doubleday, 1968).

Emblidge, David, ed. *My Day: The Best of Eleanor Roosevelt's Acclaimed Newspaper Columns 1936–1962* (New York: Da Capo Press, 2001).

Glendon, Mary Ann. *A World Made New: Eleanor Roosevelt and the Universal Declaration of Human Rights* (New York: Random House, 2001).

Goodwin, Doris Kearns. *No Ordinary Time: Franklin and Eleanor Roosevelt: The Home Front in World War II* (New York: Simon & Schuster, 1994).

Gurewitsch, Edna P. *Kindred Souls: The Friendship of Eleanor Roosevelt and David Gurewitsch* (New York: St. Martins Press, 2002).

Hershan, Stella K. *The Candles She Lit: The Legacy of Eleanor Roosevelt* (Hyde Park, New York: Eleanor Roosevelt Center at Val-Kill, 1993).

Lash, Joseph P. *Eleanor and Franklin: The Story of Their Relationship Based on Eleanor Roosevelt's Private Papers* (New York: W.W. Norton and Company, Inc., 1971).

——. *Eleanor: The Years Alone* (New York: W.W. Norton and Company, Inc., 1972).

——. *Love, Eleanor: Eleanor Roosevelt and Her Friends* (Garden City, New York: Doubleday, 1982).

Perkins, Frances. *The Roosevelt I Knew* (New York: Viking Press, 1946).

Roosevelt, Eleanor. *The Autobiography of Eleanor Roosevelt* (New York: Da Capo Press, Reprint, 1992).

———. *Tomorrow Is Now* (New York: Harper & Row Publishers, 1963).

———. *You Learn By Living: Eleven Keys for a More Fulfilling Life* (Philadelphia, Pennsylvania: The Westminster Press, 1960).

———. *On My Own* (New York: Harper, 1958).

———. *It Seems to Me* (New York: Norton, 1954).

———. *This I Remember* (New York: Harper and Brothers, 1949).

———. *This Is My Story* (New York: Harper and Brothers, 1937).

———. *It's Up to the Women* (New York: Frederick A. Stokes Company, 1933).

Somerville, Mollie. *Eleanor Roosevelt: As I Knew Her* (McLean, Virginia: EPM Publications, 1996).

Stiles, Lela. *The Man Behind Roosevelt: The Story of Louis McHenry Howe* (New York: The World Publishing Company, 1954).

Streitmatter, Rodger, ed. *Empty Without You: The Intimate Letters of Eleanor Roosevelt and Lorena Hickok* (New York: The Free Press, 1998).

Ware, Susan. *Beyond Suffrage: Women and the New Deal* (Cambridge, Massachusetts: Harvard University Press, 1981).

———. *Partner and I: Molly Dewson, Feminism and New Deal Politics* (New Haven, Connecticut: Yale University Press, 1987).

Wolfskill, George and John A. Hudson. *All but the People: Franklin D. Roosevelt and His Critics, 1933–39* (New York: The Macmillan Company, 1969).

Youngs, J. William T. *Eleanor Roosevelt: A Personal and Public LIfe* (Boston: Little, Brown & Company, 1985).

Index